ERTÉ

ERTÉ

BY CHARLES SPENCER

 Clarkson N. Potter, Inc./Publishers NEW YORK

I should like to dedicate this book to the memory of my father who, a few years before Erté's birth in St Petersburg, was born in Odessa.

This 1981 edition appears in a slightly different form from
the original American edition published by Clarkson N. Potter,
Inc., 1970.

The Library of Congress cataloged the first
printing of this title as follows:
Spencer, Charles.
Erté [1st American ed.]   New York, C.N. Potter; dis-
tributed by Crown Publishers [1970]

1. Erté
NK1535.E7S65   1970   709'.24   70-125360
                          MARC

10   9   8   7   6

ISBN 0-517-54564-0 (cloth)
ISBN 0-517-54391-5 (paper)

ACKNOWLEDGMENTS

Without Erté—in every sense—this book would not have been possible. I owe an
enormous debt to him for his unfailing kindness, enthusiasm, forbearance and
patience in giving me so much time and making available rare and precious
documentation.

  Mr and Mrs Eric Estorick of the Grosvenor Gallery have been most helpful in
allowing me access to works by Erté and to their files and records of the artist. I am
also indebted to Carla Pellegrini Rocca of the Galleria Milano, to John McKendry,
Curator of Prints at the Metropolitan Museum of Art, New York, Nancy White, the
present American editor of *Harper's Bazaar* and to Nigel Gosling and Howard Greer
who have kindly allowed me to quote from their books. I wish to thank the staffs of
the Westminster Reference Library, the United States Library at the University of
London and the National Film Institute, London; Lewinski, who took the bulk of the
photographs for this book, A.C. Cooper and Co. and Paul Watson. A special tribute is
deserved by Hilda Meyer who coped with the typing. Lastly, a special debt of gratitude
is due to Martin Battersby for his encouragement and guidance on most of the subjects
touched on in this book.

CONTENTS

AUTHOR'S NOTE TO THE SECOND EDITION

In his autobiography, *Things I Remember,* published in 1975, Erté recalls our selection for his 1967 exhibitions, "a lengthy and difficult process," during which, he kindly remarks, "My relationship with Charles Spencer became very friendly." He later refers to the launching of this book, in 1970: "I don't think I have ever signed my name quite so often, nor written so many dedications."

Happily, more than a decade later, Erté is well and active, at the age of 89, enjoying the international acclaim he so richly deserves. Since 1967 he has held numerous exhibitions in public museums and private galleries in most parts of the world. Following my own detailed study of his life and career there have been publications on aspects of his work, and a new demand for editions of his unique illustrations. The response to his original drawings in auction houses confirms the widespread recognition of his genius. Even more impressive is the evidence of his continuing creative energy in a series of new activities.

The last production mentioned in this book is the 1970 *Zizi Jeanmaire Show* at the Casino de Paris; two years later he designed sets and costumes for *Zizi, je t'aime,* well deserving a journalist's tribute, "Erté, je t'aime aussi" (*Paris Herald Tribune,* 25 February 1972). There have also been new ballets and theatrical productions, commissions for *Vogue* and other publications, posters, and designs for fashion and jewelry. The crowning event of the period was the 1980 production of Richard Strauss's opera *Der Rosenkavalier,* with designs by Erté, for the Glyndebourne Festival in Sussex, England. The enthusiastic audiences were delighted by the vitality and panache of the work of the remarkable octogenarian Erté.

There is every reason to believe that Erté has many more years of creative work ahead of him, and if this book ever goes into a third edition, I look forward to adding a further note, hopefully coinciding with his first century.

Charles Spencer
April 1981
London

Bold figure references within the text indicate color illustrations.

CHAPTER 1
AN AFFINITY
WITH THE PRESENT

Erté's talents and diligence are represented by a working career which began as a dress designer with Poiret in 1913 and continues today with contributions to fashion magazines; his first theatrical task was a costume for Mata Hari in 1913—his latest, to date, for Zizi Jeanmaire at the Casino de Paris in 1970. He has made unique contributions to the French music-hall, to Broadway, to Hollywood, to the dramatic stage, and to some of the great opera houses of the world. He has designed clothes, fabrics, shop window displays, perfume bottles, posters, jewelry, furniture, chocolate boxes, playing cards, restaurants and domestic interiors—all with the skill and modesty of a dedicated professional. Whatever the task, it has always been undertaken and completed with the same painstaking care, no matter what the subject or the purpose. And at an age when most men retire, in his seventies he took up metal sculpture and lithography.

In gathering material for this biographical study, it has occurred to me that Erté's neglect, both in the literature of the period dealing with his varied activities, and in the art world generally, is due to a number of causes. His own personality and attitude is that of a functional artist. Although a charming and friendly man, he has always lived outside fashionable or artistic movements. Living in Monte Carlo between 1915 and 1923 he remained outside the great artistic activity in Paris at that time. His main preoccupations have always been his independence and his work. Tied to publication deadlines and theatrical first nights he had little time for anything else. Except for a youthful disagreement with Paul Poiret, and a later clash with Lillian Gish, he displays none of the characteristics of temperament which breed publicity or scandal.

Another possible factor is the anonymity of his adopted name. Even in 1937, when he was famous in France and America, London theatre critics knew nothing about him and were confused by his name. One, who considered him a genius, found the nom-de-plume so mysterious that he didn't know whether to write *he* or *she*. Perhaps if Erté had remained Romain de Tirtoff, the normal sequence of a Christian and a family name might have made his identification easier.

More important, perhaps, is the effect of artistic and intellectual snobbery. I imagine it was because of this that the lavish catalogues, with excellent colour plates, for his 1929 exhibitions in Paris and New York, made no reference to the Folies-Bergère, George White's Scandals or *Harper's Bazaar* in the list of sources. There are merely descriptive titles and in some cases short literary explanations. The introductions to the catalogue and the quotations from contemporary critics avoid reference to the original purposes of the designs. The writers almost lean over backwards in their attempt to dispel the vulgar taint of printers' ink or grease paint by referring to artistic links and influences as diverse as Crivelli, Tiepolo and Longhi, Mozart, Shakespeare and Keats, Ingres and Rousseau, Baudelaire, Poe and Mallarmé, Debussy and Ravel, Outumaro and Burne-Jones. With such a lineage, artistic respectability could not be far behind! These catalogues were in reaction against the tendency to judge the purpose of art before its quality. You can be sure that a man commissioned to paint the ceiling of a cathedral will automatically be accorded greater artistic respect than some-one asked to design for the theatre—and equally you can be sure that in most cases the second kind of artist will be more professionally trained for his job. The introduction of painters into the theatre, principally by Diaghilev, has somewhat redressed the balance, but not greatly for those who function entirely as professional stage-designers; and how much less for artists active in revue and musical-comedy. Can you imagine trying to impress a typical art-gallery audience that *John Smith* who once designed costumes for the Windmill Theatre in London, or for American burlesque, is in fact a unique artist. This was precisely the reaction to Erté in New York and London—until, of course, the drawings were seen in 1967. Erté's neglect was, in fact, largely due to the fact that his drawings were not available to the public for over thirty years.

Not that one should fall into the trap of those early admirers who invoked great names in order to establish Erté's true worth; or the insistence by some recent critics that he be judged solely by the yardstick of fine art. Except for youthful portraiture and some recent sculpture Erté has never been a 'fine' artist. He has never sat at his desk, in anguish or joy, to make marks which sum up his personal philosophy or express biographical complexity, or aim to guide mankind to a new enlightenment. Erté must be judged within the range of his talents and purposes. As the English critic Andrew Causey wrote in the *Illustrated London News* (23.9.67): 'Erté's costume designs make their mark as works of art through their precision and unity of composition.'

Within his own areas of reference, Erté's drawings are perfect of their kind. They have the true magic of art, whereby a unique personality is transmitted through the alchemy of a perfected technique. This is the basis for all art, although there are degrees of ambition—and attainment (not necessarily coinciding). A label of frivolousness can only relate to the attitude of the artist, not to his subject matter. Spiritual subjects and lofty ideals are not enough; there are many instances of enduring art based on the most ordinary objects, like a kitchen pot. Given the right artist a theatrical costume can result in a statement of lasting pleasure and interest.

The revival of interest in Erté was possibly bound up with the fact that he was still alive when the 'twenties suddenly became an historical period, evoking sympathy and nostalgia, and greatest of all forms of admiration, imitation. Thus in the 'sixties Erté's drawings could be admired not only as superb examples of fashion or theatre design, or as remarkable technical achievements, or as decorative images of great elegance; they were also able to invoke the admiration of the new Pop generation who saw a romantic and desirable escapism in *Art Nouveau*, *Art Déco* and other movements of the early decades of the century.

During the 1967 London exhibition the BBC radio program *The Critics* discussed Erté's work. George Melly commented on its effect—'Particularly on art students who were swarming in there like wasps around a honey pot.' Other speakers nostalgically compared the atmosphere to 'all Odeons and Gaumonts, that whole kind of exotic oriental world that dominated architecture in the cinema'. There were references to the prophetic nature of his fashion designs, the leaning to ambivalent sexuality, which has become a feature of contemporary 'unisex'. Ernestine Carter in the *Sunday Times* (17.12.67) summed up this curious meeting of time past and time present: 'It is not just the reminder of the sumptuous past which makes Erté so interesting. It is his remarkable affinity with the present. The Black Bottom costume of 1927 might have come from any Cardin collection. The "Dance Madness" fringe of 1925 swayed a sequinned hula at Lanvin in January, and the design for a patterned stocking of 1919 foreshadowed the reality by over forty years.' A possible explanation of this phenomenon is that in the 'sixties clothes, especially as worn by young people, took on precisely that air of individualistic fantasy and fancy dress which Erté alone of the fashion illustrators of the 'twenties brought to his work.

The credit for Erté's rediscovery must be given to the French writer Jacques Damase, who met the artist when preparing a book on the Parisian music-hall. It was not merely his active presence which astounded Damase, but the fact that neatly stored away were thousands of perfectly preserved drawings representing a life's work. The immediate result was an exhibition at Galerie Motte in 1965, organized with Jacques Perrin, who the following year held another exhibition at his own gallery in Paris. Through the Motte exhibition, Erté was brought to the attention of Galleria Milano, which in 1965 included some of his work in a pioneering exhibition of *Art Déco*. The most prominent event in this sequence was Erté's inclusion in the important exhibition Les Années 25 held at the Musée des Arts Décoratifs, Paris, in 1966, which put an historical and artistic seal on *Art Déco* and the diverse artistic activities of the 'twenties.

It is fair to say, however, that complete international reappraisal only came about after the Grosvenor Gallery in London became his world agents. Jacques Damase had suggested an exhibition of Erté's work to this London gallery, to which, at that time, I was acting as an art consultant. As a result we were able to prepare his first ever London exhibition in 1967. The remarkable success it achieved was presaged by a smaller exhibition in New York a few months earlier. It had been planned to follow the London show with a similar collection in New York, based on work by Erté done for America. The New York premises of the Grosvenor Gallery were available earlier than planned and it was decided to go ahead none the less. The exhibition was received with critical rapture; among the many comments, it is worth preserving a charming remark by John Canaday in the *New York Times* (10 June 1967), describing Erté as 'an Aubrey Beardsley who mastered the Foxtrot and occasionally broke into the Charleston'. (Although I personally find the two inferences wide of the mark.) Another result of the New York exhibition was probably unique; the entire collection of some two hundred designs for *Harper's Bazaar*, American fashion houses and Broadway shows—was bought by the Metropolitan Museum of Art, through the Martin Foundation.

Even with that boost it was difficult to explain Erté's unique achievement and history to colleagues in the art world and the press in London who had neither heard of his name, nor seen his work. There were some who awaited the exhibition with interest and excitement—designers like Cecil Beaton, Norman Hartnell, Digby Morton, Alec Shanks, theatrical colleagues like Cecil Landeau, George Black, Jnr, Robert Nesbitt, and the writer and painter Martin Battersby who was already making a collection of *Art Déco* objects. The general ignorance and disinterestedness was dispelled when the exhibition opened on 19 September 1967. An indication of the remarkable interest aroused, both by the exhibits and by Erté himself, is hinted in the observation of John Russell in the *Sunday Times* (24.9.69): 'If Michelangelo were to come back from the dead he could hardly have greater or more eulogious publicity than has been accorded to Erté.'

CHAPTER 2
ST PETERSBURG

At the turn of the century St Petersburg was an imperial city of canals and ships, baroque palaces, classical façades and gigantic squares. 'A city of teeming poor, overcrowded officials and great wealth,' writes Nigel Gosling in his book *Leningrad*. 'A city of plots and gaiety, of miserable poverty, heroism, bursting artistic creation and intellectual visions . . . like a theatrical décor.' Somerset Maugham in *A Writer's Notebook* (1917), gave another view of the city: 'That you may be reminded of Venice or Amsterdam it is only to mark the difference. The colours are pale and soft. They have a quality of pastel but there is a tenderness in them that painting can seldom reach.'

It was in this romantic and exciting city, largely built by foreign architects, the capital of a vast imperial empire, that Romain de Tirtoff* was born on 23 November 1892 (10 November by the Russian Calendar), at the St Petersburg Naval School, where his father was Inspector. The Tirtoffs had settled in St Petersburg at the time of its foundation by Peter the Great, and appropriately every male member of the family since then had made his career in the Imperial Navy. The family was descended from a Tartar Khan named Tirt, one of the many tribal rulers who harassed the Russian kingdom, and under the unifying leadership of Genghis Khan invaded Europe. It was Ivan the Third, determined to establish an absolute monarchy, who subjugated the Tartar and Mongolian Khans. Erté explains that whilst many of his distant cousins bore the title of prince because their forebears had submitted to Ivan, he is only permitted the honorary use of *de* or *von* since the Tirts had to be conquered before they could be integrated into the Holy Russian Empire.

Romain's childhood was happy, comfortable and eventful. As the only son of devoted parents (his sister Nathalia was nine years older) he was greatly cherished. His mother's family, part Cossack and part Ukrainian in origin, was distinguished. Uncle Nicholas, who became the youngest general in the Imperial Army, was later appointed Military Governor of St Petersburg. Another uncle was a prominent architect, and an eighteenth-century ancestor had been a sculptor. Perhaps these precedents enabled his mother to overcome family objections to Romain's artistic ambitions.

---

* The pseudonym Erté was created from the initials R T when the artist began to work as a fashion designer in Paris in 1912. His earliest drawings done in St Petersburg were signed *Romain* or *Pitch*, a family nickname.

1 The Tirtoff family in 1905

2 Romain de Tirtoff, aged seven years, 1900

3 Graduation, 1911

During Romain's childhood St Petersburg was an elegant centre of theatrical and artistic life. At the same time, under its cultivated sophistication, ominous rumbles could be distinguished. The reign of the tough Alexander III ended in 1894 and his more gentle successor Nicholas was to be the last of the Tsars. As a child in a loyalist, aristocratic household Romain was hardly aware of political or social unrest. He was, however, thirteen in 1905 and recalls the revolutionary disturbances which caused the family to sleep in their day clothes. These followed a terrible Sunday morning when troops opened fire on a procession bearing a petition to the Tsar. Hundreds were killed. This led to the famous naval mutiny at Odessa, which included the battleship *Potemkin*.

St Petersburg was a very French city. The Franco-Russian Pact of 1892 consolidated military and cultural ties, and later brought Russia into the First World War. Two activities which deeply influenced Romain, fashion and art, were particularly dominated by France. The brilliant couturier Paul Poiret, for whom Erté was later to work in Paris, visited the city to display his creations. Modern art from abroad, principally French, was beginning to be shown in Russia in the early years of the century; great collections of Matisse, Picasso and their Parisian contemporaries, now in Russian museums, were being made by the Russian businessmen Morosov and Shchukin.

In St Petersburg there were three Imperial theatres—the Maryinsky, devoted to opera and ballet, the Alexandrinsky, with its lovely classical façade, performing Russian and foreign classical drama, and the Michaelovsky with a French repertoire and company. The Alexandrinsky, at which the great *avant garde* director Meyerhold worked as early as 1908, saw the first performance of the plays of Gogol and Turgenev. At the Michaelovsky the young Romain saw Lucien Guitry, father of the famous Sacha Guitry; within a single week he witnessed Sarah Bernhardt and Eleanora Duse each playing Marguerite in *La Dame aux Camélias*. The Music Conservatoire staged seasons of Italian opera every spring when the famous singers included Tettrazini and Adelina Patti; and for music there was the Concert Hall, with its famous restaurant, at the Pavlovsk railway station. There, in 1911, the year before Romain left for Paris, Prokofiev made his début.

The Tirtoffs were very musical. Romain's mother had studied singing, and his father, a gifted pianist and violinist, was a friend of the composer Rimsky-Korsakov. The first visit Romain ever paid to a theatre, at the age of seven, was to attend a performance of Rimsky-Korsakov's *Sadko* at the Maryinsky. The family had a permanent box at the theatre which they visited every Tuesday evening, and in his early teens Romain became a regular attendant. He gradually learned the whole operatic repertoire (most of which he was to design) and saw some of the greatest singers of the day, including Melba and Chaliapin. One of his favourites was Maria Kouznetsov, for whom he later created costumes.

Ballet made an even greater impression. The first programme he saw, at the age of seven or eight, included *The Hunchback Horse*. His enthusiasm was so great that he insisted on taking lessons—his teacher was the daughter of the great choreographer Petipa. He seriously debated whether to take up painting or dancing, and the latter remained a serious hobby. He often danced privately in Paris, on one occasion accompanied by the composer Erik Satie.

At the Maryinsky Theatre Romain saw the whole repertoire of the famous Imperial Company, on which Diaghilev's *Ballets Russes* was based. Pavlova remains for him the most memorable of all dancers. (In the 'twenties he designed a number of costumes for her solo performances.) He especially recalls the début of the young Karsavina, and what he describes as 'Nijinsky's three scandals'. The first of these was at the Maryinsky Theatre, at a performance attended by the Tsar's mother. Nijinsky, arriving late at the theatre, omitted to wear undergarments. The Royal shock resulted in Nijinsky's dismissal from the company. (The other two scandals took place in Paris—the violent audience reactions to the first performances of *L'Après-Midi d'un Faune* and *Sacre du Printemps*.) The repertoire of the Imperial Company included the great classics, *Swan Lake*, *Giselle*, *Don Quixote*, *La Bayadère*, as well as Fokine's first choreographic essays *Chopiniana* (*Les Sylphides*) and *Le Pavillon d'Armide*. Scenery and costume design was already on the spectacular scale which later astonished Europe.

It is not surprising that an artistic youth in St Petersburg in the first decade of this century should have seen his future in the theatre. The theatre, especially opera and ballet, attracted the leading young painters of the day, including Mikhail Vrubel, possibly the greatest Russian painter of the pre-modernistic period. The father of modern theatrical design in Russia was Alexandre Benois, an offspring of the brilliant foreign colony in the imperial capital. Before 1890 he formed a club of fellow-pupils who were called 'The Nevsky Pickwickians'. They were joined by a young Jew, Leon Rosenberg, who later took the name of one of his grandparents, Bakst. Another member introduced his cousin to the group—Serge Diaghilev. From these origins emerged the *Mir Iskustva* (World of Art) society, the forerunner of the whole modern movement in Russia. Soon after its foundation in 1899 both Benois and Bakst produced their first work for the theatre. The infiltration of members of *Mir Iskustva* into the Imperial theatre was due to the patronage of its director Prince Volkonsky who appointed Diaghilev as an assistant. But under Volkonsky's successor Diaghilev lost his job and was barred from further state employment. He then devoted his energies and genius to editing the *Mir Iskustva* magazine and to a series of exhibitions which introduced to Russia the work of foreign artists, Whistler, Beardsley, Tiffany, Lalique, Charles Rennie Mackintosh, Puvis de Chavannes, Monet, Degas and the Post-Impressionists. These culminated in the remarkable exhibition of Russian portraiture held at the Taurida Palace in 1905, and the Russian section at the Salon d'Automne in Paris the following year. This was the most comprehensive Russian exhibition ever held, from early icons to the young Larionov and Gontcharova. Diaghilev's ban from Russian theatrical life also led to a series of concerts in Paris in 1907, at which he introduced contemporary Russian composers, the production of *Boris Godunov* the following year with Chaliapin and costumes and décor by Benois and Golovin, and then in 1909, on May 19, the first season of the *Ballets Russes* at the Châtelet Theatre.

One of the great successes of that first fabulous season was Fokine's ballet *Le Pavillon d'Armide*, designed by Benois. The production of this ballet at the Maryinsky in 1907, writes Prince Peter Lieven, 'must be counted the first step in the direction of the Ballets Russes'. After Diaghilev's banishment, Benois had become the leading artistic influence at the theatre, and it was the success of this ballet which inspired Diaghilev to plan a season of Russian opera and ballet in Paris. As Camilla Gray writes in *The Great Experiment in Russian Art 1863–1922*, 'It is in the theatre and particularly in ballet that one must look for the creative work of the "World of Art". Here their ideals of an integrated, perfected existence, a complete realisation of life-made-art was possible.'

Erté, who saw the original production of *Le Pavillon d'Armide* in St Petersburg and the début of the young Nijinsky who danced with Fokine and Pavlova, was in every sense a child of this unique artistic evolution. He made a collection of postcards illustrating the sets and costumes at the Maryinsky and the original designs. Among his earliest existing drawings, dated 1911, are a group of exotic Beardsleyesque costumes inscribed 'For an imaginary ballet', done in St Petersburg shortly before he left Russia (figs 4, 5).

As the child of an aristocratic family he lived a sheltered life, yet there was much that must have excited his love of colour and drama; the vast royal palaces, both in the city and at Tsarskoe Selo and Peterhof, to which he was taken on excursions; the great military parades in front of the Winter Palace where 400,000 soldiers marched past the Tsar, attended by white-uniformed Guards, and the Empress in her carriage, escorted by *Gardes à Cheval* in scarlet. Then there were the special delights of winter which included troika races on the frozen river and the sight of Lapps and their reindeer from Finland camped on the Neva for the Maslanitza Fair.

Most of all, perhaps, can one trace the splendour of Erté's costumes and his ritualistic groupings of dazzling figures to the Russian Orthodox Church. With his naval antecedents Romain probably attended 'the sailors' church', the eighteenth-century St Nicholas Cathedral with its delicate columns, balconied windows and blue and white towers. At Easter the great Midnight Mass was held in St Isaac's Cathedral built in 1818, with its 144 pink columns and golden mosaic pictures between pillars of malachite and lapis lazuli. 'A marvellous Babylonian pile,' Théophile Gautier called it. Nigel Gosling recreates the scene thus:

> The Cathedral would be very dark and filled with a bluish haze of incense. In the centre, directly under the dome, lay a gilded coffin covered by the traditional silk embroidery representing the dead Christ. Round the church stood thousands of unlit candles, connected by a thread of guncotton. From behind an altar screen emerged a band of priests in black, who intoned the office of the day. A cover was placed over the silken image, and the coffin was, after inspection, declared to be empty. A procession formed up and moved slowly round the pillars looking for the missing body—eventually going out through the door to continue the search. Thus—while they were outside—a clock struck twelve. 101 guns boomed from the fortress and the great choir struck up a chorus of 'Christ is Risen!' In a flash all the candles were ignited, the great door was flung open and in poured a phalanx of clergy in gold, of choristers in blue, chanting the Easter Hymn.

4 Design for an imaginary ballet, c. 1911

16

5 Design for an imaginary ballet, c. 1911

The influence of Russian ritual and religious art, evident in all the great Russian designers of Erté's generation, was deepened by the superb collection of icons which since 1895 had been on view at the Russian Museum. The striking geometrical patterns on the vestments of priests and saints in these icons, and the shadowless linear compositions, can be compared to decorative elements in the costumes Erté designed in the 'twenties, when, after Cubism, similar dynamic shapes were fashionable.

The great Hermitage Museum was another source of Erté's artistic education; the vast collections from pre-history to contemporary art included Leonardo, Michelangelo, Raphael, Giorgione, Botticelli; the Spanish School; Flemish primitives and a magnificent group of Rembrandts. Above all, for the future designer, there were the arts of Egypt and the Far East, Scythian and Greek jewelry , collections of armour, jade, porcelain, tapestries, lace. Looking at Erté's *œuvre* there is no mistaking the influence of Greek vase painting, the precise colour patterns of Persian miniatures, the decorative suggestiveness of oriental sinuosity, the sturdy richness of the native arts of Russia.

He also saw the regular exhibitions at the Academy of Arts where the leading figures were Repin, Vrubel, Vasnetsov and Serov; and the work of foreign artists in the Diaghilev exhibitions. The modern Russian movement, however, was largely centred in Moscow and it was only after settling in Paris in 1912 that Erté came into touch with Cubism, Futurism and the other revolutionary styles which the young Russian artists adapted into Constructivism and their own forms of functionalism.

The person who most influenced Romain was his mother. Her white skin and blue-black hair remains his ideal of feminine beauty. Her intelligent informed concern for fashion and art nourished his instincts. As a small child he was already designing clothes; one drawing made at the age of five was actually translated into a garment for his mother by her resident dressmaker. The fashion magazines brought to the house, including the Russian *Damski Mir* (Lady's World) and the Parisian journals bought at the French Library, further stimulated his ambitions. With his mother he visited the elegant dress shops and milliners on the Nevsky Prospekt. He filled her empty perfume bottles with coloured water and dressed them with scraps of lace to make ballet dancers. Above all, in this respect, was the example of Poiret, as can be seen from a remarkable group of pencil sketches dated 1911 (fig. 6).

Then there were the annual visits abroad with his mother and sister. These took place between May and July, whilst his father was on naval manoeuvres. As a child he was taught English, French and German by governesses, alongside his native Russian. (Erté still speaks these languages perfectly, as well as Italian and Spanish.) His first visit outside Russia was to the Paris World's Fair in 1900. To a child of seven it seemed a wonderland: the Place de la Concorde with its illuminations and the exhibition pavilions on the banks of the Seine; the Palais de la Femme with its gorgeous costumes, and especially the wax model of the famous courtesan Marion Delorme with her long narrow face, regular features, dark eyes and black hair—the Erté ideal, which includes Marie du Plessis, the original *Dame aux Camélias*, and the Seville Madonna *La Macarena*. For these summer holidays he visited Scandinavia, Germany, Austria, the Tyrol, Hungary, Belgium, Spain, Switzerland and England. On his first visit to London in 1910 he saw Gertie Millar in Lionel Monckton's *The Quaker Girl* at the Adelphi Theatre.

After these annual visits abroad the family joined Admiral Tirtoff in August for holidays in Russia, usually at the family *ducha* near Novgorod, close to the Pushkin estate. There were also memorable trips to other parts of the country, notably, when Romain was ten years old, a cruise along the Volga to the Caspian Sea and over the Caucasus mountains to the Black Sea. The grandiose, picturesque scenery and the slim grace of the inhabitants made a deep impression, particularly the dark oriental beauty of the women and the richness of their costumes. These impressions, plus the artist's own Tartar origins, his Russian cultural heritage and the taste for orientalia in Paris at the beginning of this century, form the central core of his work.

At the age of thirteen Romain attended his first school. After a happy, fulfilling childhood it was a relatively harsh experience. He hated wearing school uniform and has never been able to reconcile himself to being part of a group. He was, nevertheless, a good pupil, passionately devoted to Russian and French literature. When he was fifteen years old the family moved to Kronstadt where his father was appointed Principal of the Naval Engineering School. (For a short period, due to serious illness, Romain's father had been forced to retire from the Navy and became a member of the Imperial Cabinet, joining his brother who was Lord Chamberlain at Court. After four years he persuaded the Tsar to allow him to return to the Navy. On leaving the Cabinet the other members presented Admiral Tirtoff with a gold cigarette case made by Fabergé, engraved with all their signatures, a memento still used by his son.)

Kronstadt was near enough to St Petersburg to enable Romain to visit relatives and attend theatres and exhibitions. In the winter this entailed crossing the frozen sea on sledges, wrapped in fur coverlets. On occasions he would stay with his favourite Uncle Nicholas, the Military Governor of the city, who each week gave a children's dance, or with Uncle Paul, the Royal Chamberlain, whose children Nicholas and Olga were Romain's closest friends. (Olga was killed during the Revolution and Nicholas settled in the United States.)

As the time approached for him to take his Baccalauréat at the age of eighteen, the question of his future loomed. Even as a child he had refused to play with military toys and it was evident to his parents that Romain was not likely to follow the traditional family callings of the Navy or Army. The Diplomatic Service, the third family career, was also declined. The question of his becoming an artist, especially one devoted to fashion or the stage, was regarded with alarm. His mother, however, prevailed, but only on condition that he studied to be a portrait painter. He had already executed a series of portraits of members of the family and a career in this genre was considered both respectable and lucrative. His mother took him to see the greatest living Russian portrait painter Ilya Repin who approved the plan and provided Romain with one of his most promising pupils, the shortlived Ukrainian artist Dimitri Lossevsky, as a teacher. After one year

6 Pencil sketches, c. 1911

Demi mondaine à la Mode.

La Vicieuse

La grue qui vent se lancer.

La Fille qui a mal tourné

19

Romain decided that his future lay in Paris. Although he had not seen the French capital since the enchanted childhood visit of 1900, it represented the mecca of all his ambitions—as a painter, as a fashion designer, as a theatrical artist. Again his mother overcame family opposition on the promise that the young man would not undertake frivolous pursuits but would enroll at the École des Beaux Arts as a student of architecture.

In February 1912 Romain de Tirtoff boarded a train in St Petersburg, armed with his first independent passport, his savings, and the promise of a small monthly allowance from his godfather Uncle Nicholas. Unknown to his family he had visited the editorial office of *Damski Mir* and arranged to send them drawings of Paris fashions, as a means of supplementing his income. Little could he or his family have imagined that the following year he would be working with the great Paul Poiret and would design his first theatrical costume, to be worn by a Dutch dancer named Mata Hari, or that within a decade his fame and success would enable him to rescue his parents from Soviet Russia.

CHAPTER 3
PARIS AND POIRET

Paris in 1912 was a fertile breeding ground for a young Russian anxious to make a career in fashion and the theatre. If St Petersburg was almost a French city, Paris was enthralled by all things Russian. This was due to Diaghilev and the fantastic success of the exhibitions, operas and ballets he had brought to Paris. It is impossible today to fully reconstruct the delirium and enthusiasm with which the *Ballets Russes* was received in Paris at the Théâtre des Champs-Elysées on 19 May 1909 and the revolutionary effect it had on fashion, decoration and the theatre. Whilst it may not have started the craze for orientalia—which had been building up in Paris since the turn of the century and had already been exploited by the couturier Paul Poiret—it was certainly the climactic event in the stylistic evolution.

In Paris Erté attended the ballet seasons of 1912 and 1913, seeing again the older items in its repertoire, as well as the new productions of *Daphnis et Chloe, Thamar*, Nijinsky's notorious *L'Après-Midi d'un Faune* and Stravinsky's *Sacre du Printemps*. A report in *Comœdia Illustré* June–July 1913 describes 'the violent interpolations against the young school of modern composers' which occurred at the première of *Sacre du Printemps*. 'Against the murmurs and sneers of the sophisticated audience assembled at the gala, representing a House worth Fr. 35,000,' it continues, 'the composer (Stravinsky) exclaimed, "they are ripe for annexation". . . . In a moment of calm a voice from the Balcony shouted "the artists cannot hear the music". It was Serge Diaghilev, with Olympian calm, who consoled the dancers and insisted that they continue.' Erté was present on that memorable night of 24 May 1913 and, indeed, at all the performances of the *Ballets Russes* he could afford. He spent hours in the museums and at the salons. He admired the work of Matisse, a few years earlier branded a 'wild beast' (Fauve), but now greatly appreciated. Picasso and Braque had introduced their Cubist masterpieces to the public at the 1911 Salon des Indépendants. In February 1912, the same month as Erté's arrival, Paris saw its first Futurist exhibition, and later that year Duchamp showed his great painting *Nude Descending a Staircase*. Orphism had been established by Robert Delaunay, and within a few years Dadaism and Surrealism were launched.

Any student of Erté's early work must be aware of his knowledge of these developments in the art of his time, which he absorbed and reflected in more popular, functional forms. (One of his earliest theatrical costumes in 1914 for the revue *Plus Ça Change* was called *La Muse Cubiste* (fig. 21). It was into this revolutionary, prophetic world of art, theatre and fashion that Erté excitedly, if timidly, entered in his twentieth year.

On his arrival in Paris he lodged at a small hotel on Rue Godot de Maurois, near the Madeleine, recommended by friends from home. It was cheap, convenient and impressively clean—he particularly appreciated the daily change of bed linen. He soon discovered that it was a *maison de passe*, where the rooms could be rented by the hour, and thus frequented by prostitutes.

He had no intention of keeping his promise to study architecture at the Beaux Arts. Instead he enrolled at the Académie Julian and studied painting under Jean-Paul Laurens, famous for his over-sized historical reconstructions. After three months he left in search of employment as a dressdesigner. He lived on his savings and Uncle Nicholas's small allowance, plus the minute fees for his contributions to *Damski Mir*. These drawings were based on clothes worn by elegant Parisiennes in the streets and cafés, and illustrations in the magazines he read at the kiosks, notably *Gazette du Bon Ton*, to which he was later to contribute, and *Comœdia Illustré*, which dealt with theatre, music and fashion. When money ran short, as it often did in that first year, hot chestnuts sold in the street proved economical and nourishing.

It took him nine months to find work with a dressmaker called Caroline in the Rue Royale. With a promise of regular income he left the *maison de passe* for a small furnished flat on the Rue des Acacias, near the Etoile. His hopes proved premature. At the end of the first month Caroline came to the conclusion that he should follow any career except that of a dress-designer. He managed to retrieve his drawings and as a gesture of defiance immediately took them to the establishment of the great Paul Poiret—his idol since the couturier's visit to St Petersburg.

Erté recalls that on 2 January 1913 he received a *pneumatique* summoning him to Poiret. The famous couturier was then at the height of his remarkable career. The son of a Parisian cloth merchant, his creative instincts had also been fanned by an early love of the theatre. In the mid-nineties he was employed by Jacques Doucet, the most famous couturier of his generation, and a great connoisseur and patron of the arts upon whom Poiret modelled his even greater fame. After a short period with the House of Worth, Poiret opened his own establishment. He was the greatest modern innovator of women's clothes, and the first couturier to publicize his work by employing gifted young artists on superb private editions. Paul Iribe and Georges Lepape, two of the finest illustrators of the period, owe their early fame to Poiret; *Les Robes du Paul Poiret* (1908) by Iribe and *Les Choses de Poiret* (1911) by Lepape are collectors' items today. They were also the prototypes for the charming covers which fashion magazines like *Vogue* and *Harper's Bazaar* used until the domination of photography in the 'thirties. (Lepape, in fact, is to *Vogue* what Erté is to *Harper's Bazaar*.)

Poiret was responsible for fundamental changes which affected woman's evolution in this century. With extraordinary instinct, allied to the expertise and elegance of a great Parisian dressmaker, he understood that modern women required an entirely different shape. The aims of emancipation, the demands which were soon to be made by the war, the greater freedom women would enjoy in commercial and social life, were all anticipated by Poiret. As early as 1904 he amazed Jean Worth with a dress based on simple vertical lines instead of decorative curves. In pursuit of a simple boyish silhouette he virtually banished the corset and fitted bodice; in the process he invented the *soutien-gorge*, now known as the 'bra', appropriately calling his first one 'liberty'. It may not come as a surprise that Colette, in the days when she was writing fashion notes for *Vogue*, objected to Poiret's 'boyish' fashions and longed for the return of 'smooth curves, the arrogant bosom and the luscious hips'.

Just how extraordinarily prophetic the Poiret pre-war look was, can be judged from the innumerable advertisements drawn by his protegé Iribe in 1912–13. The tall, thin women with their close-cropped hair and straight slim-fitting gowns in bright colours, attended by elegant young men in luxurious settings seductively lit by electric table-lamps, could, without a single change, appear in a fashionable magazine today and immediately make striking impressions.

Poiret substituted vivid hot colours for the current pastels, and introduced a feminine version of trousers. He matched the tubular Empire line with an oriental twist, harem trousers peeping from long narrow skirts. The harem skirt, or *jupe culotte*, was sometimes worn under a divided skirt separated at the knee, and even though trousers were not universally adopted, the slit skirt became essential for the popular Argentine tango. So popular in fact that in 1914 a committee of aristocratic Parisians protested against the display of too much leg. In 1912 he caused a sensation by using live models for the first time. In that year he opened his School of Decorative Art, which employed Raoul Dufy among other artists to design fabrics. Poiret was also the first couturier to market his own perfumes.

A great showman and publicist, Poiret attracted enormous attention with his 'entertainments'. The most spectacular, given in May 1911, was called The Thousand and Second Night Ball. He probably made a small fortune from the costumes he designed for the three hundred guests; those not suitably attired had to choose from a stock of Persian designs thoughtfully provided as an emergency. Poiret greeted his guests singing authentic Persian airs, and in the main salon the actor Edouard de Max recited from *The Thousand and One Nights*. At the Louis Quatorze Ball given in his house in Versailles in 1912, Poiret accompanied Isadora Duncan in an impromptu *pas de deux* to an air by Bach. For the Perroquet Ball at the Paris Opera House the guests were required to wear only shades of red and gold. Erté designed costumes for Poiret's last pre-war extravaganza, the Jewel Ball of 1913. This side of Poiret's character may also have influenced Erté, who loved making and wearing fancy-dress costumes for the annual balls held later at the Opera in Paris and the Casino at Monte Carlo.

Poiret was successful, proud, egotistical, autocratic. In his autobiography he describes an occasion when the Baroness Henri de Rothschild asked for his finest dresses and mannequins to be sent to her home. On their return the girls complained that they were made to parade in front of 'her gigolos who made unpleasant comments'. The Baroness was said to have commented on both the mannequins and the dresses: 'I knew they were ugly but I could not believe they were as ugly as that.' Poiret waited for the moment of vengeance. One day he was informed that the Baroness had arrived. He entered the salon where the parade was due to begin and informed Madame de Rothschild, 'As my dresses do not please you, I do not wish to suffer another affront in my own house and I must ask you to depart.' 'I am not accustomed to be put out of the house of my purveyors and I will not go.' 'Madame, I no longer consider myself as one of your purveyors.' Poiret then informed the rest of the company that the parade would take place in another room. The following morning an assistant nervously informed Poiret that the Baron de Rothschild wished to see him. 'Is it you, Monsieur, who put my wife out of your salon yesterday?'On its being admitted, the Baron said: 'You have done well. I know someone who adores your dresses, and she would not care to meet the Baroness here.' The lady in question became one of Poiret's best customers. In his own establishment Poiret was treated as a demi-god. A notice on the door of his atelier read: 'Before knocking ask yourself three times if it is absolutely necessary to disturb HIM.'

This then was the man whom the young Erté was summoned to meet. At that time Poiret had a magnificent establishment consisting of three private houses—on the Faubourg St Honoré, the Avenue d'Antin (now Avenue President Roosevelt) and Rue de Colisée—joined by their gardens. The carpets were gooseberry red and at the end of the principal salon, decorated with frescos, a grand formal staircase descended from the changing rooms. Here, according to Poiret, 'for fifteen years all that was subtle, Parisian and exotic in life paraded by'.

Poiret was in his early forties. A square-cut beard gave him the appearance of an Assyrian king, an impression enhanced by a splendid red and gold brocaded jacket. He had already examined Erté's drawings. The applicant was asked to do a test design and was led into a studio being used by a dark young man who was to become a close friend and colleague, both *chez* Poiret and as a designer for the Paris music-halls. It was the Spanish artist Jose de Zamora, later famous for his work at the Casino de Paris. Erté stayed with Poiret until the establishment closed at the outbreak of war in August 1914.

As a result of his new affluence Erté took an apartment at 9 rue de Civry at Auteuil, which, when he later moved to Monte Carlo, remained his pied-à-terre until 1923. Another important event of the summer of 1913 was his first meeting with a distant cousin, Prince Nicholas Ourousoff, who became his closest friend, and the brilliant business manager of the immensely successful period to come. Prince Nicholas arrived in Paris in 1913 *en route* for London where his brother, Prince Serge, married to a niece of the Red Sultan of Turkey, Abdul Hamid, had arranged Nicholas's marriage to an American millionairess. This plan came to an end at the first sight of his future wife the following spring. He returned to Paris just before war broke out.

At Poiret's, Erté and Zamora were the only full-time designers. Their drawings for dresses or theatrical costumes were usually signed by the Master. A group of unsigned sketches in *Harper's Bazaar* of January 1915, described as '. . . produced in the establishment of Paul Poiret', Erté identified as his own (fig. 7). One of Erté's first assignments was a play called *Le Minaret*, ostensibly designed by Poiret, but for which Zamora and

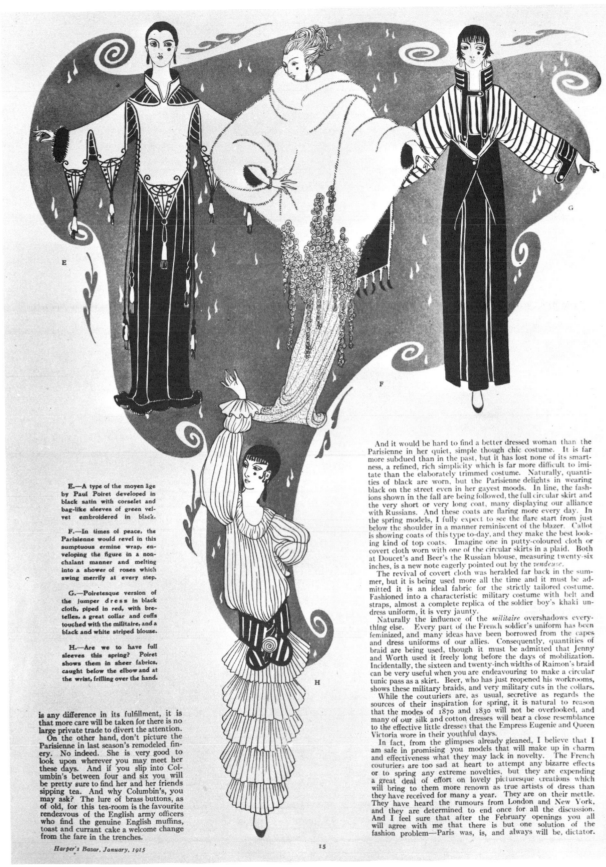

E.—A type of the moyen âge by Paul Poiret developed in black satin with corselet and bag-like sleeves of green velvet embroidered in black.

F.—In times of peace, the Parisienne would revel in this sumptuous ermine wrap, enveloping the figure in a nonchalant manner and melting into a shower of roses which swing merrily at every step.

G.—Poiretesque version of the jumper dress in black cloth, piped in red, with bretelles, a great collar and cuffs touched with the militaire, and a black and white striped blouse.

H.—Are we to have full sleeves this spring? Poiret shows them in sheer fabrics, caught below the elbow and at the wrist, frilling over the hand.

is any difference in its fulfillment, it is that more care will be taken for there is no large private trade to divert the attention.

On the other hand, don't picture the Parisienne in last season's remodeled finery. No indeed. She is very good to look upon wherever you may meet her these days. And if you slip into Columbin's between four and six you will be pretty sure to find her and her friends sipping tea. And why Columbin's, you may ask? The lure of brass buttons, as of old, for this tea-room is the favourite rendezvous of the English army officers who find the genuine English muffins, toast and currant cake a welcome change from the fare in the trenches.

Harper's Bazar, January, 1915

And it would be hard to find a better dressed woman than the Parisienne in her quiet, simple though chic costume. It is far more subdued than in the past, but it has lost none of its smartness, a refined, rich simplicity which is far more difficult to imitate than the elaborately trimmed costume. Naturally, quantities of black are worn, but the Parisienne delights in wearing black on the street even in her gayest moods. In line, the fashions shown in the fall are being followed, the full circular skirt and the very short or very long coat, many displaying our alliance with Russians. And these coats are flaring more every day. In the spring models, I fully expect to see the flare start from just below the shoulder in a manner reminiscent of the blazer. Callot is showing coats of this type to-day, and they make the best looking kind of top coats. Imagine one in putty-coloured cloth or covert cloth worn with one of the circular skirts in a plaid. Both at Doucet's and Beer's the Russian blouse, measuring twenty-six inches, is a new note eagerly pointed out by the *rendeuse*.

The revival of covert cloth was heralded far back in the summer, but it is being used more all the time and it must be admitted it is an ideal fabric for the strictly tailored costume. Fashioned into a characteristic military costume with belt and straps, almost a complete replica of the soldier boy's khaki undress uniform, it is very jaunty.

Naturally the influence of the *militaire* overshadows everything else. Every part of the French soldier's uniform has been feminized, and many ideas have been borrowed from the capes and dress uniforms of our allies. Consequently, quantities of braid are being used, though it must be admitted that Jenny and Worth used it freely long before the days of mobilization. Incidentally, the sixteen and twenty-inch widths of Raimon's braid can be very useful when you are endeavouring to make a circular tunic pass as a skirt. Beer, who has just reopened his workrooms, shows these military braids, and very military cuts in the collars.

While the couturiers are, as usual, secretive as regards the sources of their inspiration for spring, it is natural to reason that the modes of 1870 and 1830 will not be overlooked, and many of our silk and cotton dresses will bear a close resemblance to the effective little dresses that the Empress Eugenie and Queen Victoria wore in their youthful days.

In fact, from the glimpses already gleaned, I believe that I am safe in promising you models that will make up in charm and effectiveness what they may lack in novelty. The French couturiers are too sad at heart to attempt any bizarre effects or to spring any extreme novelties, but they are expending a great deal of effort on lovely picturesque creations which will bring to them more renown as true artists of dress than they have received for many a year. They are on their mettle. They have heard the rumours from London and New York, and they are determined to end once for all the discussion. And I feel sure that after the February openings you all will agree with me that there is but one solution of the fashion problem—Paris was, is, and always will be, dictator.

7 Erté's unsigned drawing of Poiret designs

8 A rare opportunity to examine the development of Erté's style; a design of 1913 – see illustration 9

9 The same design re-drawn, c. 1915

Erté produced all the costumes. 'Let me recall to you,' writes Poiret, 'the positive revolution in the art of stage presentation and design which was affected by the first presentation of *Minaret*.' With typical disdain he describes the book as poor—'The real thing was the costumes and the scenes.' At that time it was usual for fashionable couturiers to make the dresses worn by leading actresses in the theatre. On this occasion Poiret claims the innovation of supervising the entire visual effect. The play appeared at the Théatre de la Renaissance in 1913, a vehicle for the directress Cora Laparcerie, written by her husband Jacques Richepin. The leading male actor was Harry Baur, later famous in films; he and Erté collaborated again in 1929 on Edmond Rostand's play *La Princesse Lointaine*. One member of the cast was to become in her way even more famous, or notorious, than any of the other protagonists. The costumes Erté designed included one for an oriental dancer—a young Dutch woman with the stage name of Mata Hari, who was also called 'The Red Dancer' and became known for her daring performances (fig. 10).

10 Costume for Mata Hari, 1913

11 'La Muse Cubiste', 1914   12 'Le Tango', 1913

At Poiret's, Erté contributed costumes to three other stage productions. For Jacques Richepin's play *Le Tango* at the Athenée Theatre in 1913 the dresses came from Poiret's collection with some new designs by Erté. *La Revue Française Politique et Littéraire* which published a notice of the play requested two costume drawings, which somehow Erté managed to sign before they appeared (fig. 12). In 1914 Cora Laparcerie appeared at the Renaissance in an adaptation of Pierre Loüys' *Aphrodite*, for which Poiret also supervised the décor. On this occasion Erté did all the costumes. The third show to which he contributed in the name of Poiret was the Rip revue *Plus Ça Change* in 1914, for which he created the Cubist costume already mentioned (fig. 11).

Although I have referred to Poiret's habit of signing the work of his employees, he was nevertheless responsible for the first appearance of the signature 'Erté' in a fashion magazine, probably its first professional appearance in France. The leading fashion magazine in Paris was *Gazette du Bon Ton*, superbly printed in colour, employing the finest French fashion illustrators. Erté's name appears in the issue for May 1913, under two charming designs for hats with an article entitled *Le Ruban* by Drésa. There are six other unsigned illustrations by him. A possible explanation for Poiret's recommendation of the young artist to the editor Lucien Vogel may be found in the fact that with the article there is also a full-page colour illustration by Georges Lepape, Poiret's protegé and collaborator. It may be

29

13 This is probably the first appearance
of Erté's signature in France

that Lepape had seen Erté's work *chez* Poiret, or had asked his friend to recommend an artist to do the drawings (fig. 13).

An interesting point arises from a study of *Bon Ton*. In most cases the drawings of new fashions appear as dramatic or narrative situations. Thus we find such titles as 'God—but it's cold' for Lepape's drawing of a superb red brocade winter coat by Poiret. Two gentlemen raise their hats as a carriage departs, in an article on men's coats, with the exclamation: '*Tiens—already on their way home.*' 'The Mouse' is the title for a scene showing a frightened lady in a tailored costume by Doucet; another lady, elegantly dressed by Redfern, pouts in annoyance, 'My guests have not arrived.' One of the most charming captions accompanies a drawing of a flowered afternoon dress by Paquin—'Say nothing,' the wearer whispers as she takes a note proffered by a hand at her balcony.

This literary tradition Erté inherited, and affectionately embraced. His fashion models are often depicted in anecdotal situations, whilst the sentimental or moral insinuations of his covers for *Harper's Bazaar*, as I shall explain, led to the printing of his explanations. This need for depicting costume as part of a dramatic situation was to be more fully manifested in his work for the theatre.

By the time war broke out in August 1914 Erté had spent eighteen months with Poiret. He had not only witnessed the workings of the greatest dress house in Paris but had come under the influence of one of the most extraordinary and gifted decorative artists France has produced, whose daring taste, perfectionism and deep respect for the importance of design, no matter how ephemeral the object, were to be of lasting value in Erté's career. He also learned the methods and requirements of designing for the stage. For the immediate future, he took from Poiret a knowledge of fashion magazines and dress houses in the United States, which together form the arena of his first independent success. His inexperience, however, led to a parting clash with Poiret, which resulted in permanent animosity. (This may account for the fact that although Poiret's biography *My First Fifty Years* was written in 1930, by which time Erté was renowned, his former employer does not mention his name once and certainly does not reveal that costumes for the four shows mentioned were contributed by Erté. It must also be said that in Erté's essay on Modern Dress in the 1929 *Encyclopaedia Britannica*, so important a figure as Poiret is conspicuous by his absence.)

Finding himself in need of work, Erté teamed up with one of Poiret's leading dressmakers in an attempt to sell dresses to the American market. They printed cards which gave their names 'Erté et Adrienne', the latter described as a former *première de Poiret*. Poiret took legal action to prevent the use of his name. Erté paid damages and never spoke to Poiret again.

Despite this setback the partnership succeeded. Their first client was Henri Bendel, owner of the famous New York store (figs. 71, 72). For the annual influx of American buyers, Erté and his collaborator prepared a collection and called on Mr Bendel at the Hotel Normandie. They sold him thirty dresses. Later they had similar success with another important New York fashion store, Altmans. In subsequent years Erté designed for many American clients.

Public events determined Erté's future as a fashion designer—not along the path of an exclusive couturier, but as an artist selling drawings to retail and wholesale houses in the United States, and shortly afterwards to *Harper's Bazar*, one of the most influential American organs of fashion. At the outbreak of war France had little immediate need for the chic dressmaker; nor could it offer Erté employment in the theatre. As a result he became famous in the United States before he was well known in Europe.

14 Erté's second cover for *Harper's Bazar*, 1915

CHAPTER 4
MONTE CARLO AND HARPER'S BAZAAR

Erté moved to Monte Carlo in 1914 after an illness sufficiently serious to bring his parents to Paris. As a result, his father spent part of the war years as a prisoner of war in Germany; his mother, who returned to Russia later, had to travel via Scandinavia. He did not see his parents again until he brought them out of Soviet Russia in 1923.

With his cousin Prince Nicholas, Erté lived in Monte Carlo until 1923—commuting regularly to Paris. It was during the early days of his convalescence that Nicholas suggested that he send some designs to *Harper's Bazar*. His first contribution, which appeared in January 1915 (also containing his unsigned Poiret drawings), was a cover characteristically entitled *Schéhérezade* (fig. 73). In March, *Harper's* printed the first of a regular series of illustrations under the title *Les Modes Creées à Paris*. By the October number the magazine claimed 'Erté's sketches are done exclusively for Harper's Bazar', with the boost: 'This famous designer is acknowledged to be one of the cleverest in Paris. His designs are full of practical suggestions and show original and charming details.' The following month his second cover appeared (fig. 14). The December issue contains two pages of illustrations by Erté. Thus by the end of the first year with *Harper's* he had already established a reputation.

The magazine at that time used such famous illustrators as Bakst, Drian, Dulac, Brunelleschi and Georges Barbier. Its chief contributors include Elinor Glyn's sister, Lady Duff Gordon, who wrote on and illustrated fashion under the name of 'Lucille'; Lady Randolph Churchill contributed a regular feature, usually with such staccato titles as 'Discipline', 'Extravagances', 'Benevolence'; another favourite writer was the Countess of Warwick who advised on 'The art of Staying at Home', 'Health and Hair', recommended 'Breathe Deep', or proposed 'A Chat about Corsets'.

Erté continued to contribute to the magazine in 1916, but in that year *Harper's* closest rival *Vogue* also used his drawings. The first appeared in the issue of 15 June 1916. On July 15 *Vogue* announced 'That original artist Erté, who not only draws costumes but designs them, forecasts the motorists of the near future'. Further contributions appeared in the numbers for August 1 and 15, by which time *Harper's* became worried and approached Erté with a ten-year exclusive contract. His work did not appear in *Vogue* again until after the success of his London exhibition in 1967.

In April 1917 *Harper's* printed a photograph of the artist with the caption: 'The foremost designer of original fashions in the world. Facsimile repro-

Designs from Paris
by
ERTÉ

Who but Erté could conceive of sleeves so long that they loop about the full velvet train and a girdle that is all points and tassels? The front of this sumptuous opera coat differs but little from the back. The tassels are there and the fur bands, but the lower edge of the skirt is several inches from the floor.

Extremely high backs or startlingly low fronts are distinguishing features of Erté's designs. This dancing frock, all silver, green and blue, possesses the quality so typical of the artist. Drapery pointed down and an overskirt pointed up hang over a short narrow petticoat of silver tissue. Earrings, bracelet, ring and bird are all part of the picture.

A single button fastens the redingote of blue-green velvet and holds in place the muffler that began as a collar. Cuffs of skunk that might be individual melon muffs and a jockey cap are touches that lend charm to the costume. As for the skirt, it is short and, like the redingote, lined with orange satin which turns over the edges in a border.

Harper's Bazar, January, 1916

15 Page from *Harper's Bazar*, 1916

ductions of Erté's drawings appear exclusively in *Harper's Bazar* every month.' In fact from January 1915 until December 1936 he contributed to 264 issues, of which 240 carry his covers. In twenty-one years he made over 2,500 drawings for the interior pages. Altogether his long association with *Harper's* represents one of the most important departments of his immense output.

Harper's Bazar, originally a weekly, was founded in 1867, as 'a repository of fashion, pleasure and instruction'. Fletcher Harper based its name and content on *Das Bazar*, using the original fashion plates of the Berlin magazine. *Harper's* was bought by the International Magazine Company in 1913, but not until 1929 was the Germanic spelling of its name changed to 'Bazaar'.

By joining the staff of the magazine Erté became an employee of the remarkable and notorious William Randolph Hearst (1863–1951). Hearst's desire to make the magazine sophisticated and gay was achieved under the editorship of Henry B. Sell (1920–26) who also maintained the literary character of the original publication; his contributors included Arnold Bennett, Compton Mackenzie and Robert Hitchens. Later editors with whom Erté worked were Arthur H. Samuels and Daisy Fellowes.

At the age of twenty-four William Randolph Hearst was given the San Francisco *Evening Examiner* by his father, who had bought the paper for political purposes, after making a fortune in silver mining. This was the beginning of Hearst's vast newspaper empire—created largely out of rivalry to Joseph Pulitzer —and his introduction of what is called 'yellow journalism'. By 1922 he owned twenty daily papers and eleven Sunday papers in most of the largest American cities, plus six magazines including *Harper's Bazar* and *Cosmopolitan*. Erté contributed to both these as well as to *Woman's Home Journal*, a Sunday newspaper supplement. Hearst in fact pioneered both the colour supplements and comic sections of American Sundays. One of his methods was to engage the best staff by outbidding other employers, and, on the whole, giving them the opportunities to use their talents. Erté was always treated with courtesy and respect by Hearst and his editors. Once you were on Hearst's payroll and regarded as his protegé, you were boosted, to your own and your employer's greater glory. (Erté's career as a film-designer owes much to Hearst.)

Hearst's less attractive methods are illustrated by two famous stories. In New York he originally rented space in the building used by Pulitzer's *Sunday World*. When Hearst decided to publish his first New York paper he used this 'wooden horse' to seduce his landlord's entire staff, who literally changed bosses in one day—a triumph for Hearst's cheque-book. Frank Luther Mott, the historian of American journalism, suggests that if Hearst had not challenged Pulitzer to a circulation race the Spanish–American war might not have occurred. Bent on stirring up trouble, and news, Hearst sent a reporter and illustrator to Cuba. The artist Frederic Remington cabled back that everything was quiet, that there would be no war, and that he wished to return. Hearst's famous reply was: 'Please remain stop you furnish the pictures and I'll furnish the war.'

16 'Oiseau du Nord', 1916

17 'Le Silencieux', c. 1916

18 'J'en ai Revé', c. 1916

Eventually Hearst lost interest in his publishing empire and concentrated on films, as a result of his infatuation for Marion Davies. His extravagances led to financial difficulties, especially after the depression, and in 1937 he was forced to abdicate control over the less important publications, which included *Harper's Bazaar*. Carmel Snow who took over the editorship in 1933 was determined to alter its character. She appointed as art editor Alexey Bradovitch who, according to an article in the 100th Anniversary Number in 1967, 'wanted the magazine to read like a sheet of music. He and Carmel Snow would dance around the paper before them on the floor trying to pick up the rhythm.' (Clearly the inspiration for the Fred Astaire–Audrey Hepburn film *Funny Face*.) This article also explains that 'He and Miss Snow, over Mr Hearst's objections, soon replaced the covers of Erté with others, and then a torrent of photographers'. Thus Erte's fate with *Harper's* was tied to that of his boss and admirer, William Randolph Hearst. When the latter's control ended, so did Erté's contract. He did not in fact meet Hearst until 1925 in Hollywood. In 1921, however, he received a letter from him introducing Mrs Hearst who came to Paris where Erté designed clothes for her (figs. 19, 20).

19 & 20 Designs for Mrs William Randolph Hearst, 1921

It would be wrong to regard Erté's fashion drawings for *Harper's Bazar* as dressmaker's designs in any ordinary sense. They are essentially ideas and inventions, full of typical touches of fantasy and the idiocyncratic use of materials—extensions, as I have suggested, of his sense of drama. His unique qualities were quickly recognized by the editor. The issue of 15 November 1915 bears a demure photograph of the artist on the Contents Page and the explanation:

> Erté's name has long been familiar to *Harper's Bazar* readers through the original costumes that he designs exclusively for this magazine, but few know that he is Russian by birth. His love of colour is the heritage of his race, and this combined with the inspiration he receives from his adopted country, France, makes him one of the most remarkable artists of his day.

Alongside his drawings there is a further editorial note:

> In the January 1915 issue of *Harper's Bazar* Monsieur Erté began to contribute his extraordinary designs for *Bazar*. At first his eccentric drawings were not fully understood by the public and his ideas were criticized as impracticable. But to those who are able to interpret his charming originality and develop in fabric and garniture his clever ideas, Erté has been an inspiration.

Critical, or at least quizzical, comment obviously continued, for in January 1918 a not dissimilar explanation is given:

> Some people look at Erté and say they have never seen women with faces like those he draws. Others say his drawings are wonderful, but his styles are too extreme. . . . The great ability of Erté is in his fertility of ideas . . . the designer of one of the best-known New York houses told me the other day he has obtained more ideas from Erté's drawings in *Bazar* than from any other source of fashions.

Erté constantly made it clear that he was not concerned with merely being fashionable. In an autobiographical piece requested by the editor and printed in March 1919 (fig. 21), he explained:

> I do not recognize the mode. I love the luxury and beauty of fashions and I believe that feminine clothes should serve to adorn woman's charm . . . in short woman's costume should be individual. The mode is more or less routine matter. But you say it changes frequently, yes, but it makes me dislike to see during a whole season women of all types in crinolines or perhaps in tight skirts. . . . I have not followed the trend of fashion but among my creations each woman can select something suited to her, without adhering strictly to the mode. . . . Just consider how boring it would be if during the whole season you met women all of the same type who said the same things, had the same ideas! I experience the same feeling when I see women dressed alike. That is why I do not like the mode which in its efforts to create a paradise of feminine beauty, succeeds in producing just the opposite effect. I am individualistic in my creations of feminine fashions.

ERTÉ WRITES HIS OWN BIOGRAPHY

Dear Mr. Editor:

YOU have asked me to give you for Harper's Bazar a few lines about myself. I do this with great pleasure.

I was born in 1892 within the walls of the Naval School at Petrograd. My father, then Captain, at present Lieutenant-General—retired since the Revolution—belonged to the Navy. My late uncle was Naval Minister, and all the members of our family followed, through tradition, this noble outdoor career.

I am one of the few members of my large family of sailors who, because of my health when a child, have not followed this career. But I have retained a fervent love for the sea, for its great open spaces, which I always hold dear and which frequently inspires me.

I passed the greater part of my childhood surrounded by the sea in the forts of Cronstadt, where my father was Commandant of the School for Naval Engineers. I studied at the College of Cronstadt, and after my graduation I resolved to give myself up entirely to my passion for painting.

To be perfectly frank, painting has fascinated me more than any other study ever since my childhood. I remember that when I was five years old I already drew, and the creation of feminine costumes interested me very much. But it was necessary for me to busy myself seriously with drawing in order to succeed in a life of art. I set aside landscape work and had the honor of becoming a pupil of the celebrated Russian painter, S. E. Repine, in the portrait field. I worked with my master at this kind of painting for three years, and I made a certain number of portraits. Meanwhile I did not forget woman's dress, for my imagination had not stopped working along this line, and when I was fifteen I was a contributor to a fashion magazine in Petrograd, in which my creations appeared with almost every issue.

This little success of mine in my own country did not dampen my desire to go on studying painting. Quite to the contrary a strong determination to work, and to go far along the road of art, was born in me. I remembered always the words of Goethe, who said that "real talent is composed of nine-tenths work and one-tenth genius." I (Continued on page 102)

21 'Erté writes his own biography', *Harper's Bazar*, 1919

That, he certainly was in the thousands of drawings reproduced in *Harper's*. They include not only delightful and extraordinary ideas for dresses, coats and hats; there are inventions for beach wear, masks, muffs, shoes, jewelry (for almost every part of the female anatomy), hat pins, veils, gloves, bags, umbrellas, luggage. Displeased by the old-fashioned layout of the magazine he soon produced complete pages, rather than single drawings, which enabled him to set elegant ladies in modernistic interiors, with personal suggestions for furniture, lamps, cushions, window-boxes, gardens. What makes this unceasing flow of ideas even more impressive is the precision of the drawings, in which his firm, steely line is matched by exquisite detail. It is not surprising that his monthly contributions earned gushing editorial admiration: 'Who but Erté could conceive of '—whatever. it was; 'To cut leggings as part of the skirt is Erté's privilege'; 'Erté's originality is always surprising'; 'The foremost designer of original fashion in the world'; for a gown named *Musique Passionnée*, '. . . an amusing name but everything Erté does is entertaining'. Certainly Erté's drawings were always entertaining, often naughty and amusing, sometimes caustically depicting unfortunately plump ladies trying to come to terms with current styles.

An unknown side to Erté is revealed in his contributions to *Harper's Bazar*. As I have indicated before, an element of theatre is never absent

22 Muff, 1922

23 & 24 Bathing Costumes, 1922

25 'Chapeau Eventail', 1921

26 Two masks, 1921

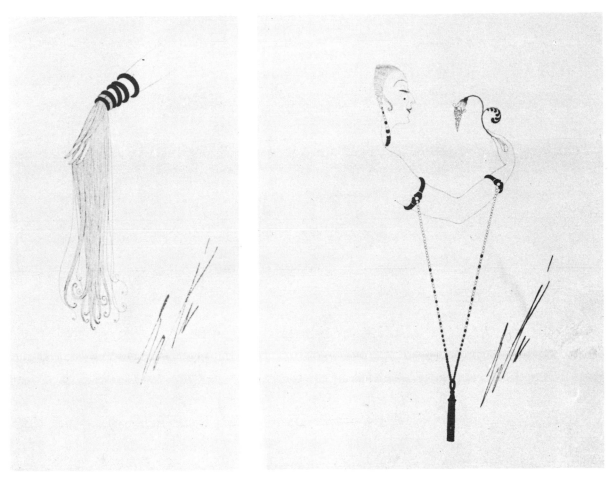

27 Three designs for arm jewelry, 1922 and (below) 1924

28 Head-dress, 1921

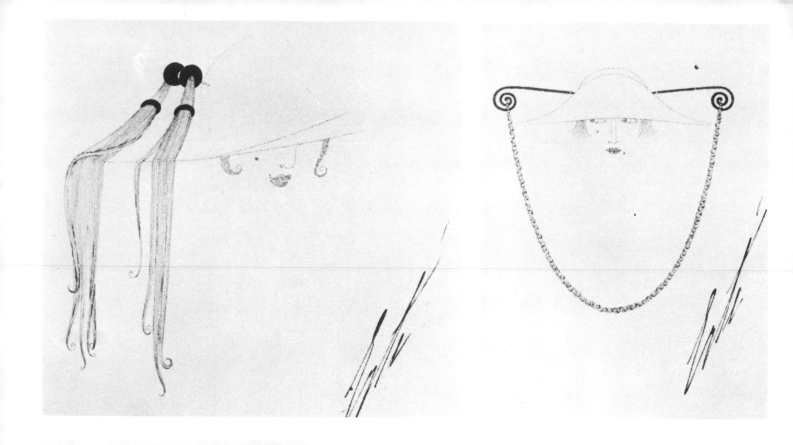

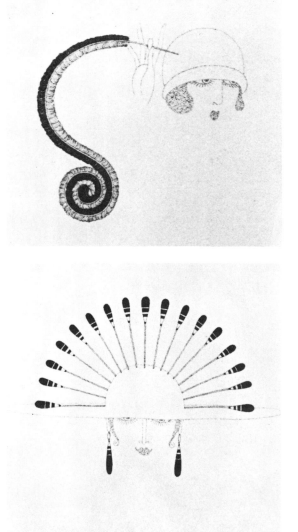

29 Four hatpin designs

30 'Chapeau pour le soleil', 1922.

31 'L'Eventail – Face à Main d'Erté', 1922

32 Tortoiseshell comb, 1922   33 Ivory comb, 1924

THE
IMPROVISED CAGE

ERTÉ'S description of this
month's cover, translated
from the French

My imagination has taken me, this time, to a shady park, where summer sings its love songs with the buoyant warbling of birds. To relieve the heat, there is a fountain in the center of an open space, outlined in silhouette against a background of sun-bathed foliage. Two little girls, in light frocks, have left the cool shade of the trees, in pursuit of a beautiful bird. At last they plan a way to capture it. They let the water of the fountain overflow so that, falling like rain over the edge of the bowl, a cage is formed, inside of which flutters the bird, taken captive. Then, indeed, they are quite happy.

But, though the pleasures of childhood pass, recollections of such pleasures linger long in the memory, and grownups often use the same ideas for their amusement as do children. My thoughts follow one of these little girls who enjoyed capturing the bird, and I now see her on one of the first steps of life's staircase, in a beaded crinoline, under which she has imprisoned two lovers. Of course, it is not difficult to escape from this thin skirt, nor was it difficult for the bird to leave its watery cage. But the bird will fly away with its bright plumage wet, while the lovers can save themselves, but with broken hearts.

HARPER'S BAZAR
JULY, 1922

34 & 35 Frontispiece, *Harper's Bazar,* July, 1922, and opposite, the costume based on the above drawing worn in the Greenwich Village Follies, 1922

from his fashion drawings. This is particularly true of his covers for *Harper's* where despite seasonal requirements, he could indulge in fantasy and drama. In the early covers the scenes are often architectural, virtually stage sets, even fetishistic in their use of chains and suggestive imagery. They are certainly anecdotal and must have demanded explanation. The issue of January 1918 states:

Your *Harper's Bazar* this month is graced by the most significant allegorical cover Erté has ever conceived. It represents the spirit of France awakening sleeping America. The crowing cock portrays France. The woman is America. The spirit of France, as yet unscathed by the hungry flames, typifying the German invasion, is warning America to abandon the bed of gold on which she has been asleep in fancied security—rousing her to action before the flames shall attack her as they have attacked Europe.

The editorial writer was clearly infected by the playful eroticism never far from Erté's work.

From April 1919 he was given regular space on the Contents Page to explain his cover designs. Very soon these explanations take the form of Wildean moralities. The cover for August 1919 is called *The Enchantress*:

A beautiful woman, forced by her parents' watchfulness to meet her lover secretly, signalled to that cavalier to join her at night by placing a flower garland upon the wall. And thus by candle and lantern light they met many times at the cupid statue in the old park, until one day he was called to war. . . . On his return, rejoicing in her loyal love, he sought the garden wall. On it, to his surprise, he found a garland. He wondered—'How can she know I have come?' . . . That night in joyous anticipation, he hastened towards the trysting place. Suddenly he saw a light. 'It is

47

she' he exulted. But then a second flame appeared, joining the first. . . . Alas I cannot tell how the story ended, for a breeze snuffed the lights and all was darkness.

Even the Christmas cover, December 1919, entitled *Once on a Christmas*, is given an ironic twist. A young girl holds a vanity box whose mirror reflects a kissing couple:

> She sees behind her two people embracing under the mistletoe. Certainly 'he' has no right to indulge in this pastime, but she turns with horror to see the awful reality, unable to believe even the mirror. Terror shows in her eyes and she drops the powder-puff from her hand. Alas! The mirror never lies.

One of his most characteristic conceits accompanies *Love's Captive* in December 1921 (fig. 37):

> A young girl has left the Christmas Ball in her blue coat embroidered with flowers of orange, beautiful both because of her faultless *toilette* and her youth. . . . Suddenly she realises a blizzard is threatening. The only refuge on the road is an old temple of love. . . . All night the wind whistles and soon long icicles begin to hang from the temple's roof. With sunrise she decided to leave but finds herself imprisoned by the icicles which form a cage about her, binding her to Cupid.

1924 saw a change of style; the symbolic imagery almost vanished, and with it the necessity for Erté's little moral tales. Instead of richly gowned, rather oriental, ladies in elaborate boudoirs or theatrical décors, the figures on the covers are simplified to humorous visual ideas. It was the advent of the flapper whose clothes in primary colours were less fussy, less formally or consciously elegant. Although Erté's name is often regarded as synonymous with the 'twenties, he was never completely sympathetic to the new age and its fashions. He once confessed: 'I didn't like it personally, although in a way it was my most productive period. I preferred the pre-war things, the long elegant line.' In fact he found himself more in tune with the fashions of the 'thirties and Dior's *New Look*.

Significantly, in 1926, with the end of Henry Sell's editorship, Erté stopped contributing fashion drawings to *Harper's*. He continued to design the covers but these became stylized in an entirely different idiom, influenced by Cubism, often based on severe, geometrical patterns, with no hint of the mildly erotic fantasies or the moralistic sentiments of earlier years (figs. 38–41). He continued to illustrate literary contributions by Richard le Gallienne, Lord Dunsany and others.

There is another unexpected side to Erté's association with *Harper's Bazar*. In addition to the cover explanations which appeared from April 1919 to the end of 1923, he also contributed over a number of years a personal letter or diary commenting on life in France. These commenced in May 1919, perhaps as a result of the success of his autobiographical piece in March of that year. Almost all of these articles are signed from Monte Carlo. In March 1921 the address is given as 'Villa Excelsior, Rue de la Source, Beau Soleil, A.M.', to which he had moved at the end of the previous year; and in May 1924 he writes from '124 Rue de Brancas, Sèvres,

36 'The Unfeeling Heart', *Harper's Bazar* cover 1918

37 'Love's Captive', design for a *Harper's Bazar* cover, 1921

38 *Harper's Bazar* cover, 1924

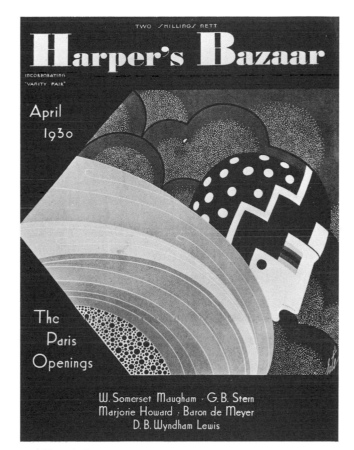

39 *Harper's Bazaar* cover, 1930

41 *Harper's Bazaar* cover, 1933

40 *Harper's Bazaar* cover, 1935

THE WORLD OF FASHION RETURNS TO THE
BEAUTIFUL SPAS OF FRANCE

A chair of green lacquer encrusted with silver and upheld by silver balls is one of Erté's delightful ideas. Its cushion of green velvet is striped with silver.

Monte Carlo, August, 1920.

Mon cher M. Editor:

MONTE CARLO is once more deserted, for the season is completely at an end. The foreigners, so numerous during the winter just past, have abandoned this corner of Europe for the brief seasons in the mountains or on the sandy beaches of the ocean.

The government of the principality, always considerate of its foreign guests, has thought it necessary to facilitate the departure of its winter sojourners by opening to them at the *Palis des Beaux Arts* an ethnological survey of the French watering-places. One has but to visit the exposition attentively in order to be able to choose a place for rest or health where one may best pass the summer months.

The war and above all peace, which have left the doors of the frontier almost closed to pleasure travelers, are bringing about a change in the habits of invalids and voyagers; instead of going to foreign spas, it is the French resorts which are now profiting, and the public knows that France is not less rich in all which concerns mineral waters than are the other countries of Europe. It is of the utmost necessity to find in France itself spots for repose and cure, for even Switzerland, so near and so desirable formerly, is absolutely inaccessible now to travelers from France, owing to the exchange; in order to expend one thousand francs in Switzerland one must carry with him two thousand five hundred francs of French silver. That is why this summer the spas of France will be filled to overflowing with a gay throng. The tourists are beginning finally to explore the French Alps in default of the Swiss Alps, and they will see Alpine beauties unknown to a large part of the public.

Then, Monte Carlo is empty. But in this momentary calm it is accumulating strength for the coming season, which promises to be even more brilliant than the one which has just ended. Even now there is not a villa or apartment to be had for the approaching winter, and one can not but foresee a great influx of sojourners.

The weather continues to be superb, and nature is fresher and more beautiful than during the season. I really pity those who must depart. The gray mists, which the winds and surf bring in as they pound upon the sandy beaches of Brittany and Normandy, could never rival the vivid colors of the Mediterranean. This southern sea becomes as calm and tranquil in the summer-time as the life upon its shores, and smiles at the blue sky above from its sparkling billows. The eyes and the souls of those who remain here in summer are

42 & 43 Erté's letter from Monte Carlo, September 1920

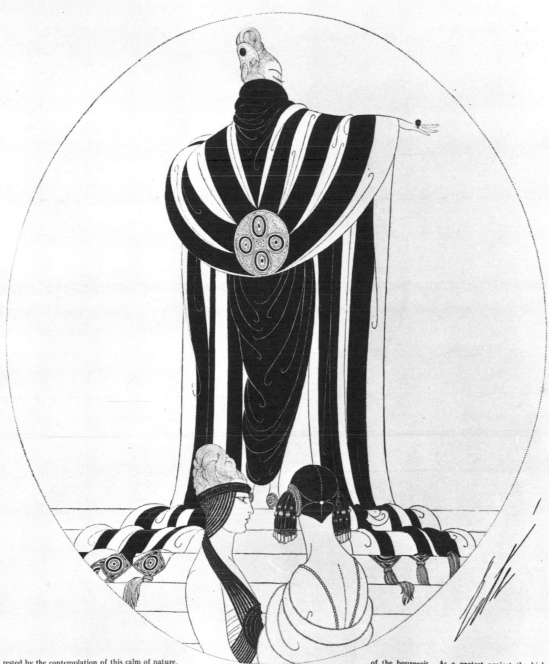

rested by the contemplation of this calm of nature.

All the distractions and all the attractions of the season are forgotten. Those who stay on are searching for amusements in other and less worldly pastimes. One may see popular itinerant shows which go on almost without interruption during the entire summer at Monte Carlo. Then one may see at Cannes the ravages caused to the best properties of the vicinity by the ant called Argentine, and one may contemplate dead fruit-trees and kitchen-gardens, every plant and weed of which has been gnawed by these minute enemies of the laborious farmers.

The bourgeois have their own amusements; they don the "salopette" (the workingman's costume of blue linen) in order to combat the high cost of living. This costume, associated with physical toil, which one is used to see spotted, soiled, saturated with perspiration and sometimes with blood, now promenades the streets of Nice

Triumphant in Erté's sleeveless manteau du soir of deepest black satin—Madame extends her arms in ecstasy. There is a soft rustle when she walks, as two long strips of satin, striped with gold, trail upon the floor. These, attached by a motif of golden embroidery, form the sleeves.

and Paris fresh, crisp and spotless. One sees it often worn by a man who would be incapable of driving a nail; and the laborer on his return at nightfall in his citizen's clothes, his work over for the day, stops nonplused before this crowd of blue phantoms and laughs slyly at this game

of the bourgeois. As a protest against the high cost of living, one dons the livery of the working-man, of the workingman who has contributed so largely to the costliness of living, and one marches across localities indicated as being in the range of the apparatus of the cinematograph, and one says to oneself—"We are few in number, but the films of the cinema will spread our audacious innovation throughout the entire country." But is it an innovation—a new French mode? No, it must be at least four months since this infantile protest, born in America, crossed the ocean and arrived in France. I do not know what form it took in America, but here it took a ridiculous form. I have seen at Monte Carlo an individual in a "salopette" made of heavy silk with a match-ing hat. For this absurd outfit he had paid more than for a complete costume made by a leading tailor. I have seen, as well, several people arrayed in the ordinary "salopette" seated about the gam-

44 Evening gown, 1917

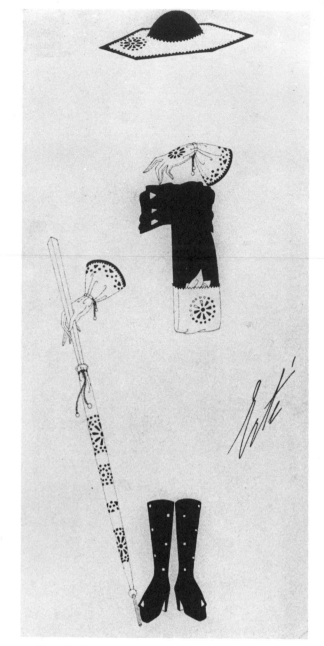

45 'Pour le Promenade', 1918

46 Evening coat, 1921

47 Designs for mink capes, 1921

France' marking his departure from the Côte d'Azur. The 'letters' do not necessarily refer to the illustrations accompanying them. They are personal commentaries on the artistic and social life on the coast, with references to new fashions, and occasional notes on events in Paris. Many of these comments have a lively period flavour and there is often an unexpected asperity in his views. Indeed when I read some of them aloud to him—after fifty years—he remarked: 'I don't think I would say that today.' Here are some characteristic excerpts:

When you meet in the streets of Paris a celebrated actress wearing a hat with an enormous French Coq upon it you think it's amusing. . . . But when you are shown at the couturier's a 'victory exhibit', it's a shock to you to realize that victory has already been commercialised. (May 1919.)

The ex-Empress Eugénie is already installed in her villa at Cap Martin, the King of Montenegro is cited among recent arrivals, the Shah of Persia is expected. . . . (February 1920.)

The new Archbishop of Paris, Cardinal Dubois, announced himself against 'fashions contrary to the decent Christian' and against dances. The war, which is finished, has shown us a great many women who seem to pass all their time in ephemeral pleasures . . . yet in those humble years accomplished formidable achievements. And who dares to say now that they are not Christian if at present they wear the new 'décolletées' toilettes. . . . (April 1921.)

Writing about the new 'exotic' dances, including 'the Shimmy':

Who would have thought five years ago that we should be dancing during lunch, afternoon tea, dinner and supper. The mania for dancing, like every other mania, grows to a certain point of its development and then declines. The statistics show us that 242 new dancing salons were opened in 1920. Perhaps the present year will open one thousand more new dancing salons, and then little by little the public will weary of this amusement and demand the right to eat quietly in the restaurants. (April 1921.)

. . . what a strange fate is mine! During the summer to think of costumes for winter and during winter of spring clothes. Never to live the life of a season during that season, but to be continually a herald of the mode. (December 1921.)

I will not conceal from my readers that I am very fond of masked balls and I love dressing myself in costumes created by me and for my own self personally. (May 1922.) (See figs. 48, 49, 50.)

Who are all these polite-looking young men with pale faces, like the faces of Irishmen coming out of English prisons—they are the professional dancers attached to this great restaurant of the Casino. (May 1922.)

It was certainly his work for *Harper's Bazar* which made Erté's name well known in the United States and which helped to promote his career as a

49 Erté dressed as an Egyptian Momie, 1923

48 At the Bal du Grand Prix, Paris Opera, 1926

50 Erté as 'Clair de Lune' at the Monte Carlo Sporting Club, 1922

Broadway designer, and later his trip to Hollywood. An indication of his rise to fame is illustrated in a rather charming, naïve book written in 1918 by Ethel Traphagen, a teacher of fashion who had worked on Hearst's *Women's Home Journal. Costume Design and Illustration* is a simple manual for the would-be designer: 'It is well to have the student really know what a good line is . . . for this purpose have examples of different kinds of good and interesting lines such as Japanese prints, some reproductions of good line drawings by McQuin, Erté, Dryden, Drian, etc.' Later in the book the student is urged to become familiar with the work and methods of such artists as 'Drian, Brunelleschi, Barbier, Lepape, Erté'. Miss Traphagen illustrates Erté's work with designs from *Harper's*, including a splendid pair

51 'l'Amazone du Demain' and 'Promenade Matinale', 1916

52 Evening dress, 1924

54 Three dress designs, 1924

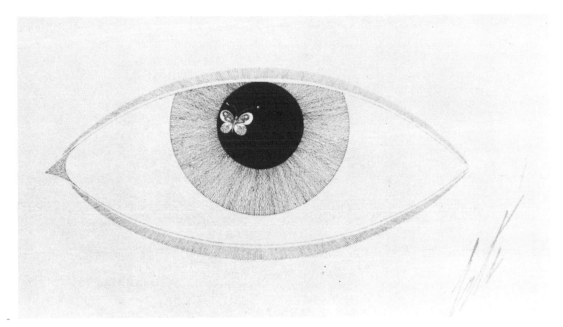

53 Drawing for frontispiece of *Harper's Bazar*, 1923

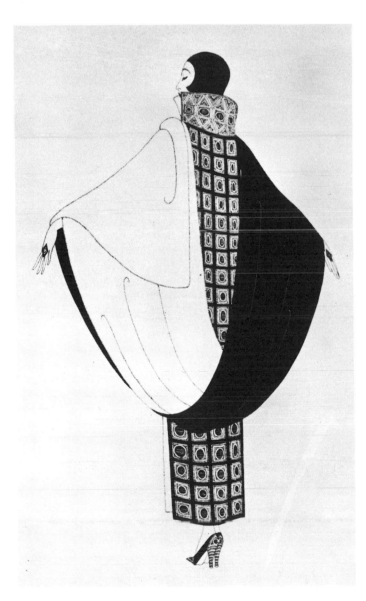

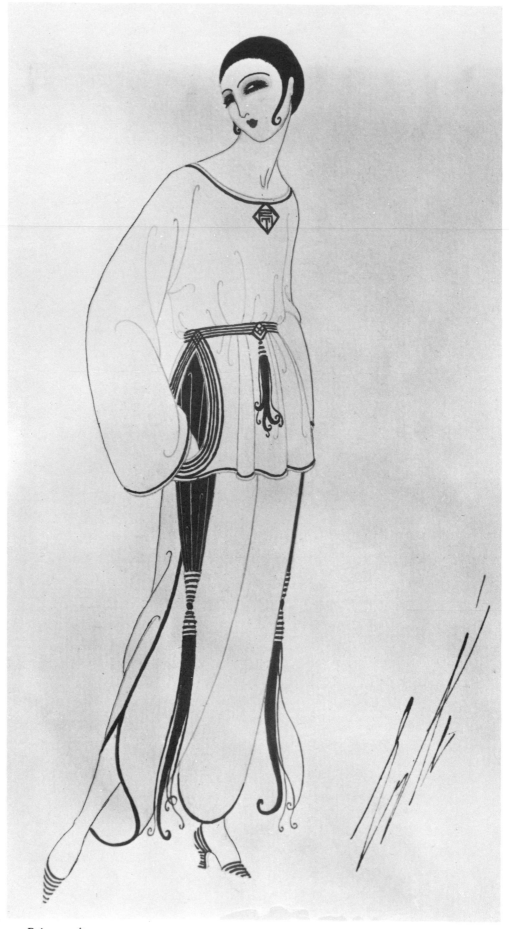

55 Pyjama suit, 1922

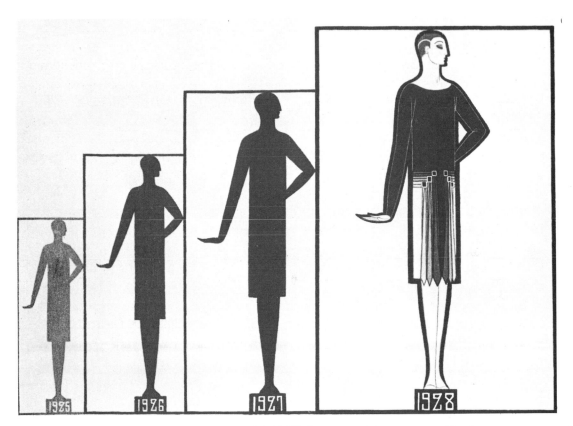

56 Silhouettes 1925–28

57 'Modern sports dress for men and women', 1929

of mounted ladies in somewhat fetishistic jodhpurs—with the comment: 'The drawings of Georges Barbier, Lepape and Erté all show the influence of Aubrey Beardsley.' (See fig. 51.)

Some years later he was asked for a series of illustrations on 'The Changing Silhouette in Women's Dress' for the 14th edition of *The Encyclopaedia Britannica* (1929),* as well as an article on 'Modern Dress', which appears on pages 656–8, signed 'R de T-E'. For this article he uses drawings to demonstrate changes in style between 1923 and 1928 (figs. 56, 57). He describes the period from 1914 to 1920 as the 'least notable in the history of fashion'. Of the flapper styles of 1924 he writes: 'Traces of the masculine influence will remain in feminine costume for a long time since woman has adopted two articles from man's wardrobe—the sweater, and the pyjama.' Characteristically, he notes a reaction in 1928 and appears to welcome the more feminine, lengthened skirt.

Before closing this chapter, it should be recorded that Erté continued to design clothes into the late 'thirties and has been regularly commissioned to design jewelry, shoes and various accessories. As an illustrator his work has appeared in the French magazines *Art et Industrie*, for which he designed covers and illustrations in the 'twenties and 'thirties, *L'Illustration*, *Fémina*, *Le Gaulois Artistique*, *Plaisir de France*; and the English journals *The Sketch* and *Illustrated London News*.

* Warren Cox, the art editor of *Encyclopaedia Britannica* who commissioned Erté, later opened an art gallery on Madison Avenue, New York, and put on Erté's first important American exhibition in 1929.

CHAPTER 5
THE MUSIC HALL

Erté's rise to fame, the revelation and exploitation of his talents, among which the capacity for sheer hard work is not the least important, coincide with the economic boom between 1920 and 1930. 'Everybody's Doing It. Doing What? Getting Rich' is how Marvin Barrett categorizes the 'twenties in his book *The Jazz Age*. A typical article in the Hearst press was called 'Everybody Ought to be Rich'. Women in particular were encouraged to spend as an expression of their new independence. The columnist Dorothy Dix outlined the new American philosophy: 'The old idea used to be that the way for a woman to help her husband was by being thrifty and indust-rious . . . but a domestic drudge is not a help to her husband. She is a hindrance. . . . A man's wife is the show window where he exhibits the measure of his achievements. . . . Good looks are a girl's trump card. . . . Dress well and thereby appear 50 per cent better looking than you are. . . .' The great spending spree, epitomized by William Randolph Hearst, changed the concept of popular entertainment, particularly the three forms in which Erté was to work with such distinction—the spectacular French revue, its Broadway equivalent and the movies.

There can be no doubt that his deepest ambition was to design for the stage. From the moment he reached Paris he spent any spare money on visiting the theatre, the *Ballets Russes*, the opera, the music-hall. Two productions were of special significance for his future style. In June 1913 he saw Ida Rubinstein in one of the historical dramas written for her by Gabrielle d'Annunzio, *La Pisanelle ou la Mort Parfumée* directed by Meyerhold, with dances by Fokine and designs by Bakst. It was set in Cyprus in the Middle Ages, with the actor Edouard de Max playing the Prince of Tyre. Even more prophetic was Max Reinhardt's Deutsches Theatre production of *Sumurun*, based on stories from the *Arabian Nights*, which came to Paris in late 1912 or 1913, after being seen in London. It was done entirely in mime, with little scenery but gorgeous costumes by Ernst Stern in riotous colours and strange shapes. This kind of oriental pantomime was the theatrical form adopted by French revue, the visual splendour largely dependent on magnificent costumes, which either in the opening tableau or the finale, or both, built up to elaborate and daring ensembles. In this genre Erté was to become a master.

As we have seen, his first opportunities in the theatre came through Poiret. His real chance came from Madame Rasimi, one of the pioneers of French music-hall. She had taken over the Ba-ta-Clan Theatre in 1910 and in 1913 was offered the directorship of the New Middlesex Theatre in

London. This was after her revue *J'adore Ça* was brought over by Oswald Stoll so that British audiences could see a complete French show. The *Daily Mail* described it as a 'kaleidoscopic spectacle of eighteen scenes with everything necessary to give pleasure to the eye and ear'. Another of her early revues at the Ba-ta-Clan is described in *Comœdia Illustré* as being 'dressed in 500 sumptuous costumes which affirm the prestige of Madame Rasimi, and 30 décors which the scene painters have made most ingeniously'. She was an impresario with the taste and experience to recognize Erté's promise.

In 1915, living in Monte Carlo, and making his first contributions to *Harper's Bazar*, Erté was asked to design *La Fête de St Cyr* (fig. 58). These annual shows at the famous military school were highly professional affairs. The cast included the actor de Max, who a few years earlier Erté had admired in the d'Annunzio drama, and the young Yvonne Printemps.

Designs for this show were shown to Madame Rasimi by her daughter who lived in the South of France and knew Erté. Thus in 1916 he was invited to contribute to a revue at the Ba-ta-Clan; his numbers included *Les Amazones* (fig. 59), a characteristic mixture of antique and oriental motifs, and a group of costumes called *Modes Excentriques*, a genre which was to become another speciality when he later worked with the costumier Max Weldy at the Folies-Bergère. In 1917 Madame Rasimi put on a famous revue *L'Orient Merveilleux* at the Fémina Theatre, starring Mistinguett and Maurice Chevalier (repatriated from a German prisoner-of-war camp), with Lucienne Vedoux and Harry Baur (whom Erté had worked with in 1913). For *Miss* he designed a series of magnificent gowns and cloaks, and the first of the giant head-dresses (fig. 61) with which she later became identified—copied, it must be said, from Gaby Deslys. For that show Erté also produced his first completely oriental extravaganza *The Thousand and Second Night at Baghdad* (perhaps inspired by Poiret's famous ball) (fig. 60). Two drawings reveal yet another facet of his theatrical manner already formed: *Diamond Statue* (fig. 62) is made entirely of jewels strung on a series of spiders' webs, with scroll motifs outlined in diamonds; *Genii of the Lamp* (fig. 63) wears gold lamé harem trousers with strings of pearls linking up different parts of the costume. This use of complex jewel-strung shapes, and their extraordinary simulation on paper by the use of raised dots of gouache or metallic paint, is one of Erté's best-known stylistic signatures. For *Gobette de Paris*, at the Ba-ta-Clan that year, he designed a ballet *Légèreté*, and some daring costumes for a number *Fleur du Mal* (fig. 64) in the Beardsleyesque manner of his youthful efforts in St Petersburg.

Two years later, at the Fémina, he worked with the greatest French music-hall star of her day, Gaby Deslys. She had returned to Paris in 1917 from the United States, with a fortune in jewels and the first American jazz band to appear in the French capital. For *La Marche à l'Etoile* at the Fémina, Erté produced one of his most magnificent scenas, *Les Rois des Légendes* (fig. 75), which in the elaboration of the costumes, the daring colour combinations and the statuesque dignity of the figures, is on the same high level as his first film designs that year.

In *Histoire du Music-Hall*, Jacques Feschotte writes: 'The music-hall,

58 Costume designs for *La Fête de St. Cyr*, 1915

59 Costume design for *Les Amazones*, 1916

60 'The Caliph's Favourite', 1917

61 Costume for Mistinguett in *L'Orient Merveilleux*, 1917

62 'The Diamond Statue', 1917

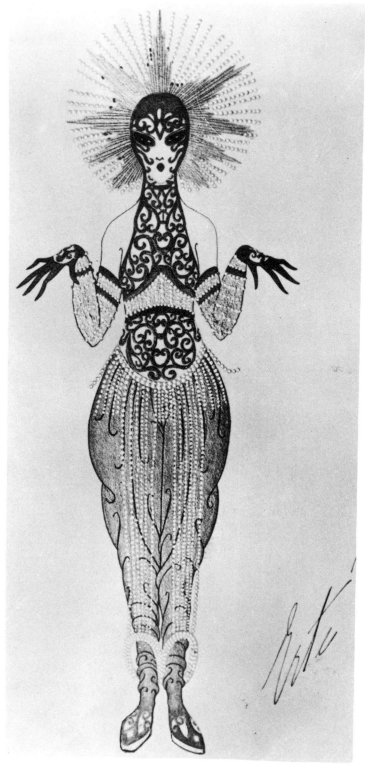

63 'The Genie of the Lamp', 1917

70

64 Cactus costume for *Fleur du Mal*, 1917

already very brilliant between 1900 and 1914, reached its apogee in Paris between 1919 and 1935.' It was in fact in 1919 that Erté started a long and successful career with the Folies-Bergère which was to last throughout this golden era.

The origins of the Paris music-hall lie in the *café-concert*, just as the English music-hall evolved from pub entertainments. In 1869 the Folies-Bergère became the first music-hall in Paris, based on the London Alhambra. Seventeen years later it mounted a prototype revue. Its early stars were Yvette Guilbert, Löie Fuller, La Belle Otéro, Liane de Pougy and Fred Karno's Troupe with the young Charlie Chaplin. After Mistinguett, its second great woman performer this century was Josephine Baker, the girl from St Louis, Missouri. She first appeared at the Folies in 1925, after the triumph of the *Revue Nègre* the previous year, which was, according to Jacques Damase, 'as revolutionary as the *Ballets Russes*, and like it a subject of violent controversy'. During Erté's decade with the Folies the other great stars included the female impersonator Barbette (Van der Clyde), known as the 'jazz age Botticelli'; Raimu, a singer from Marseilles who was to become famous in the plays and films of Marcel Pagnol; the Hungarian girls known as The Dolly Sisters; Fernandel, one of Mistinguett's partners; Jean Gabin, who started as a chorus boy in 1912; Arletty, whom Erté first met when she was a model with Poiret, and before she changed the final 'e' in her name.

Apart from its great stars the French revue became synonymous with nudity and spectacle—and as the work of Erté and his contemporaries Gesmar, Ranson, Zig, Zamora, Brunelleschi, Colin, proved, in the hands of gifted designers bare flesh could become an integral and undisturbing part of ingenious decorations.

The origin of strip-tease is said to be the Bal des Quat'z Arts of 1893. The annual fête on the Left Bank was attended, as usual, by artists, students, models and prostitutes. On this occasion the personal attractions of two girls were debated by their admirers. The girls then stood on tables for their ankles to be judged. Competition extended to their legs, thighs, hips, buttocks, breasts, shoulders. One girl ended up completely naked. The next day she was fined by the police and in protest the students of the Ecole des Beaux Arts staged a two-day revolt. The affair of Mona's nudity received so much attention that an astute music-hall director realized he had an attraction at once new and easy to stage. Thus in 1894 the Divan Fayon put on *Le Coucher d'Yvette*. Since a woman could not be shown nude on the stage, or even in a state of *deshabille*, the audience were invited to watch the artiste progressively undressing. As Paul Derval, the historian of the Folies-Bergère, put it, 'the imagination is always in advance of reality, so to the audience the young lady was nude long before she had slipped off her last clothes'. This was the beginning of a public phenomenon (it had happened in private, of course, many times) which not only characterizes the French music-hall, but is now one of the attractions of urban civilization. The first time that a woman appeared completely nude on the French stage was at the Casino de Paris in 1919.

Spectacle as the prime ingredient came after the First World War. The post-war boom promoted lavish spending on clothes, personal and domestic decorations, and public entertainments—the three main outlets in Erté's early career. After 1917, writes Jacques Damase, came 'the reign of the nudes, the sumptuous décors, the reign of the electrician, the engineers, the maître du ballet; the reign of the stars and of elaborate stage machinery'. The evolution of the music-hall towards costly spectacle resulted in a new importance for the orchestra, the introduction of shapely girls, both as dancers and clothes-horses, and especially the need for rich and picturesque tableaux. In the process the French revue arrived at the unlikely mixture of erotic symbolism and sexlessness (particularly noticeable in the work of Erté), whilst investing popular entertainment with great taste and elegance. It is therefore not surprising to find an authority like Jacques-Charles, for many years one of the most original revue directors, giving pride of place to the designer as the star of revue.

If the designer was one of the vital creative forces, the costumier was one of the principal technicians. In Erté's theatrical career, the second important figure after Madame Rasimi is Max Weldy. The role he played in revue is indicated by a comment of Paul Derval, one-time Director of the Folies-Bergère: 'The artistes are a façade, a beautiful façade, but behind the décors is a little unknown world, . . . concerned with curtains and costumes. The fabrics required for a revue measure some 500 kilometres—the distance from Paris to Lyons; 17 kilometres of ribbon are needed to execute a special curtain. There are two workshops for costumes, one occupied with maintenance and the other making new dresses.' In charge of this unknown world at the Folies-Bergère was Max Weldy. (The same age as Erté, he is said to be still making theatrical costumes in Florida, USA.)

It was during the régime of Paul Derval that Erté was asked to work for the Folies-Bergère. In 1919 he contributed two scenes, a huge show piece based on Venice in the eighteenth century (fig. 65), and for a ballet *Fonds de la Mer* (fig. 66) a group of witty costumes for octopus, lobster, goldfish, rayfish, etc. This was the beginning of an amicable association which lasted until 1930. Erté readily admits that much of his rapid international fame was due to Max Weldy. In his workshops and studios Weldy made all the costumes and scenery for the Folies-Bergère. He also executed copies ordered by theatres throughout the world.

An article in *Paris Soir*, 18 December 1928, describes how 'Max Weldy, from his office, controls the studios which furnish the entire world with revue, ballets, operettas and musical comedies. Two or three hundred persons work here every day. . . . I opened the despatch ledger, one revue is at the Cape, others at Calcutta, Bombay, Shanghai, Hong Kong, England, at Oslo, etc. Current commissions include a revue costing one hundred thousand dollars for the USA. Costumes, décors, curtains are exported by Weldy to the Winter Garden, to Ziegfeld, to the Apollo Theatre New York; also to the Admirals-Palatz or the Grosser Spielerhaus at Berlin, the Olympia at Barcelona, the Queen Victoria Madrid, the Maypon at Buenos Aires. For Paris Weldy mounts each year the revues at the Folies-Bergère. That means a million or a million and a half costumes each year.' It was through Weldy that Erté's designs were seen all over the world within a few years of his joining the Folies.

With his great expertise Weldy was able to guide Erté, and in his turn

65 Venetian costume, 1919

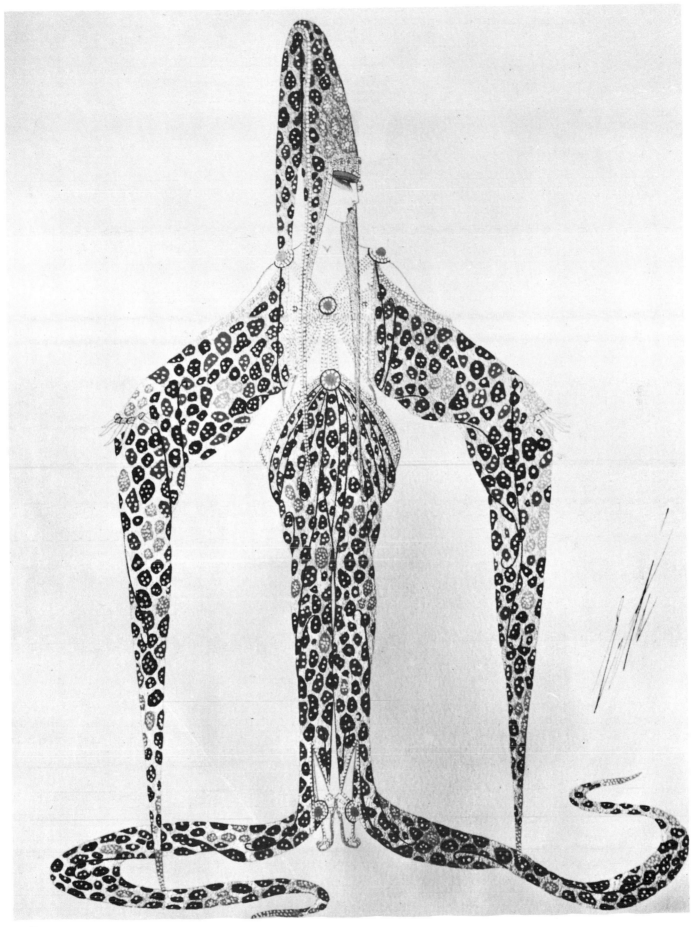

66 'Starfish' *Fonds de la Mer*, 1919

Weldy appreciated not only Erté's fertile imagination and inventiveness but his complete grasp of dressmaking and theatrical techniques. Erté had enjoyed a thorough training *chez* Poiret; now he studied with scientific thoroughness the architecture of the theatre, the structure of the stage, the possibilities and limitations of stage machinery and lighting. For his demanding tableaux and scenic effects he learned to use to the utmost the theatre's equipment. He was also able to suggest scenic effects previously unknown.

Working in an ephemeral medium, Erté's early theatrical work is known today only through his surviving designs. The perfectionist manner, resulting from a complete mastery of technique, and the small scale precision of the compositions do, of course, express his own character. But they also make for an unfailing functional style. In other words, everyone concerned, from the backer of the show, the producer, the performers to the costumier, wig-maker, jeweler and stage hands, could see exactly what was expected of them. Since his bosses were, for the most part, men of limited artistic education, they were delighted not to have to puzzle over expressionistic or abstract sketches, no matter how brilliant, in order to arrive at a picture of the desired effect. Similarly, Weldy and his craftsmen must have found Erté the perfect colleague since they too did not need to interpret, but merely to copy. These finished images were, in fact, backed up by working drawings, made by copyists, with detailed instructions on the making, materials, colours and decorative means.

The principal difference between Erté and other leading designers for the French music-hall, apart from the extraordinary length of his activity, is that whilst the theatrical result of their work may have been as effective, the designs they left behind rarely have Erté's fastidious completeness as images. One of the reasons why his original designs exist in such abundance is that he himself valued them. If they left his studio he made determined efforts to ensure their return, but in most cases it was the work of copyists which went to dressmakers and scene painters—so carefully done that even today they are often confused with, and sold as, originals.

In his autobiography Howard Greer, who was later to become famous as a dress-designer in Hollywood, describes an attempt, in 1920, to obtain employment as one of Erté's copyists. With an introduction from Madame Rasimi's daughter in Monte Carlo, Greer was invited to visit the artist:

Erté's villa was high on a hill overlooking the Casino and its surrounding gardens. A fiacre met me at the station. A servant in striped green-and-white vest, with black satin sleeves, opened the door of the villa to me. I was shown into an enormous well-lighted room, where the only furniture was a huge, neat desk, and a chair, placed directly in the centre of the black-and-white marble squared floor. Around the walls a grey-and-white striped curtain was hung from a height of five or six feet. Erté came into the room. He was wearing lounging pyjamas, which I suspected were made of ermine. A gigantic Persian cat arched its back against his calves, gliding in and out between his legs as he walked towards me. Prince Ouroussof, trailing a dressing gown of Chinese brocade, entered majestically. We discussed my proposed job for a few strained moments.
      'Would you like to see some of my sketches?' Erté asked, and, stepping

67 'Messalina', 1923

towards the wall, pulled a cord, and all the lengths of grey-and-white curtains separated, disclosing hundreds of framed drawings hung in precise rows. There probably never existed a more prolific or immaculate artist than this diminutive Russian, who spent his days and nights over exotic, slant-eyes ladies writhing under masses of fur, birds of paradise, and pearls. He took up from his desk the drawing that I was to copy. I noticed for the first time the methodic neatness of his desk. A fat bowl stood in the centre, sprouting several hundred brushes of varying length and size. Erté opened a top drawer and showed me its contents. Dozens of jars of tempera paint in every conceivable tone of red. The drawer beneath it held as many jars in varying tones of blue. Below that were drawers of yellow, purple, all the hues of the rainbow. No matter what shade he wanted, it was ready mixed for him.

When I left the villa, clutching the drawing under my arm, I was cautioned both by Erté and the Prince of its great value. I returned to Cannes and spent three days of conscientious work upon my copy. When I went back to Monte Carlo with it, Monsieur Erté was dissatisfied. 'We will forget all about our plans' he said lightly.

A desk similar to the one Greer describes, with brushes of varying length and size, and drawers containing dozens of jars of paint in every conceivable tone, occupies the artist's present studio. He is a nocturnal creature, preferring the night and early morning. He works under a brilliant electric lamp, surrounded by almost complete blackness. This symbol of concentration illustrates his need for uninterrupted periods of complete quiet. The final designs take days to complete, and they represent the laborious end of a long process of sketching, planning and mathematical calculation. Magazine illustrations, such as those for *Harper's Bazaar*, are usually drawn in pen and ink; in the theatrical designs even the thinnest, most sinuous or extended line is painted with a brush.

Even as a youth in St Petersburg he used gouache, adding metallic paints in gold, silver and copper to suggest splendour or drama. Over a working life of sixty years the methods have not changed, although they have been perfected. The meticulous detail, which is among the special qualities of an Erté design, never becomes oppressive. The anxiety to describe precisely is enlivened by an extraordinary skill in rendition and a lightness of touch which matches delicious wit with charming elegance. It is interesting to contrast the realistic detail with the dreamlike fantasy of the whole. An indication of his need to both translate his ideas into exact visual terms and to make them fully understood as theatrical effects, is the suggestion of three-dimensional elements. In his almost obsessive use of jewels Erté virtually invented a laborious, almost nerve-racking method of over-painting on tiny areas—a process repeated until a kind of mini-relief is achieved. This is but the ultimate example of the dedication, concentration and patience which form the foundation of Erté's art.

Apart from the quality of Erté's designs as works of art, or their functionalism as blue-prints, there may be another reason for his success in terms of theatrical effectiveness. We have already noted that both Poiret and Erté loved to make and wear fancy dress. There is a common involvement in fantasy, in make-believe, in unreality, in their work. Less so in Poiret's activities as a couturier, since he was selling clothes to be worn; but his obsessions with the colourful orient and the theatre bear out the suggestion. Erté's fashions in *Harper's Bazar*, by his own admission and the comments of the editor, had little to do with practicality. He is more an illustrator than a designer of clothes to be worn. Dressmakers have told me that his drawings are so precise that they could make up his ideas without any further instructions; but both in the manner in which they are presented and in the playful near-surrealism of the details, there is an inescapable air of fantasy. Much more so in the theatre where the purpose was escapism and spectacle. Here he designed for a non-stop Fancy Dress Ball with himself ever present; it may not be too far-fetched to suggest that the absolute conviction of his imaginative processes and the certainty of their translatability into theatrical reality, lies in the fact that he was, in a sense, always designing for himself.

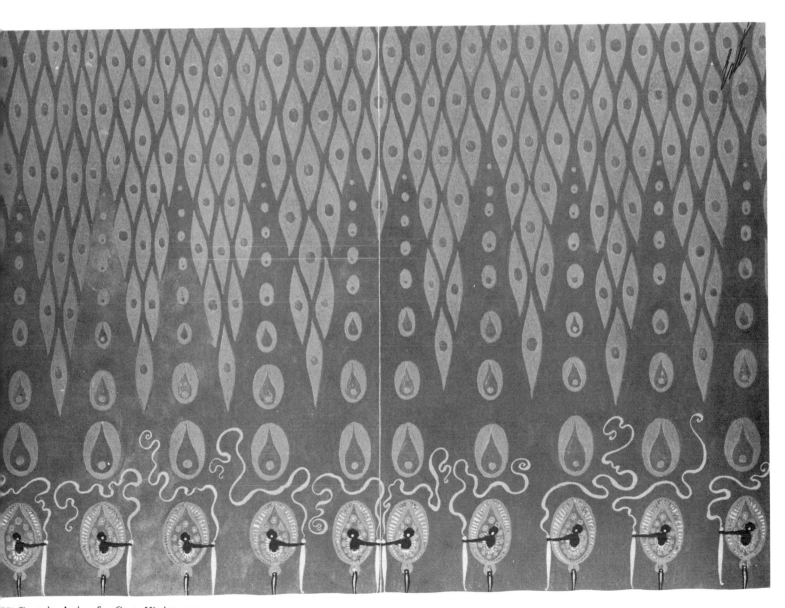

58 Curtain design for *Conte Hindou*, 1922

Reviewing Erté's 1967 London exhibition, the art critic John Russell made a meaningful observation: 'Erté is saved . . . by the quality of his involvement.'

Erté's designs for the Folies-Bergère are among his finest work. Outstanding, in my view, is *Conte Hindou* (1922). The costumes and décors represent a ravishing sequence of colour and form, completely free of banality, never repetitious and endlessly inventive in the smallest details. Some of the designs with their patterned fabrics and curious side movement (a favourite device this for attendants), are reminiscent of the drawings of the Viennese artists Klimt and Schiele, although there is no evidence that Erté knew their work at the time (figs 76, 77, 79, 80).

When *Les Idoles* (figs 81, 84, 85) appeared in 1924, René Bizet wrote in *Candide*, 'Monsieur Erté has a number of perfect tableaux, colours chosen with taste; the delicateness of his historical liberty reveals extravagance

69 & 70 Costumes, *Conte Hindou*, 1922

71 Evening coat, c. 1916

72 'Splendeur', c. 1916

74 'La Toilette de la Nature', design for a *Harper's Bazar* cover, 1920

73 Erté's first cover for *Harper's Bazar*, 1915

75 'Le Roi Sage Gasper' 1919

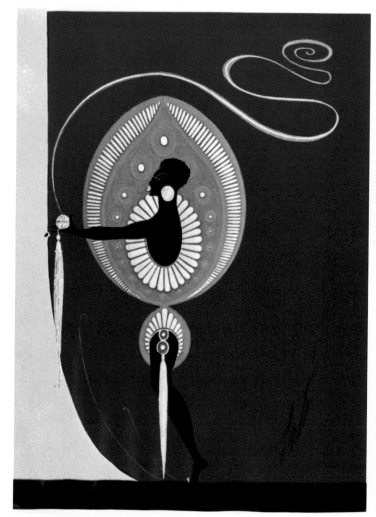

76 Curtain design for *Conte Hindu* showing detail

77 'Plume', 1920

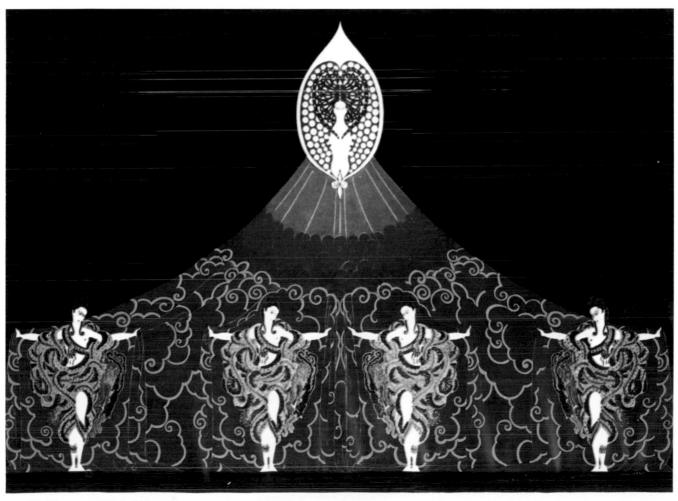

78 *The Treasures of Indo-China*, 1922

79 Venetian Courtesan, 1923

80 Schéherazade decor, 1929

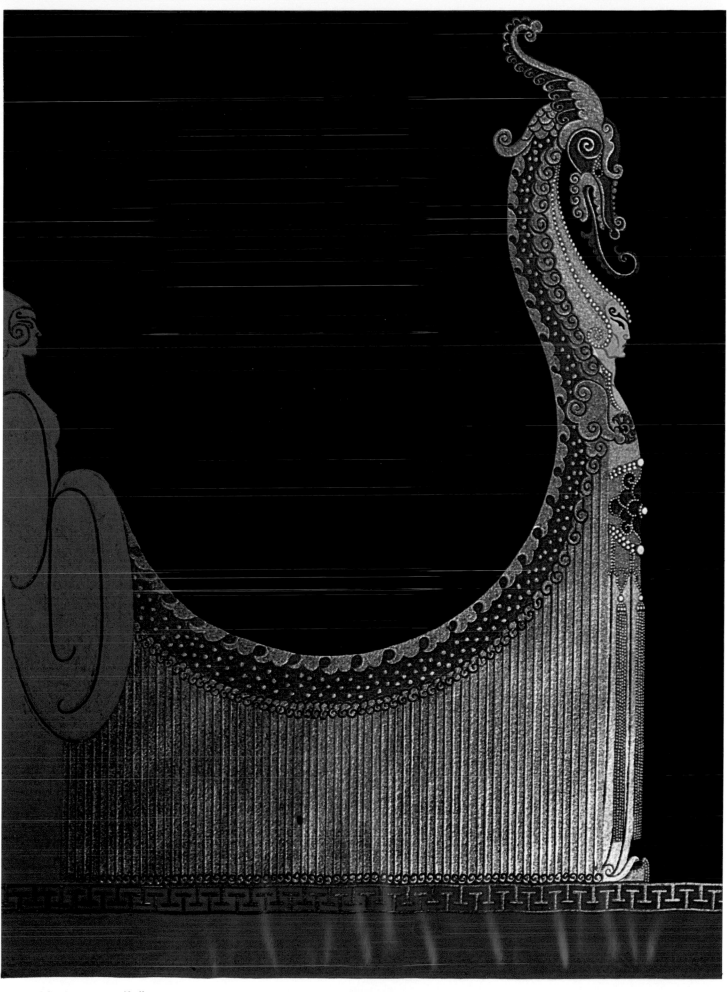

81 Wedding costume, *Aladin*, 1929

82 Melisande's attendant in *La Princesse Lointaine*, 1929

used with intelligence.' It was another item that year, *Les Bijoux des Perles* (fig. 86), which *Le Figaro* described as 'a gleaming showcase in which young women in tasteful *déshabillé* represented rings, bracelets, earrings, pendants and clasps'. These, like the spectacles at the Alcazar de Marseilles (probably part of the Weldy empire), *Les Trésors de l'Indo-Chine* (figs. 78, 87, 88) and *Au Reveil du Passé*, and *Les Baisers* at the Fémina (figs. 89, 90), at about the same time, represent Erté as the oriental or historical specialist. It was his mastery of such thematic material which led to his engagement on the first straight play since his Poiret apprenticeship—*Le Secret du Sphinx* (fig. 91) by Maurice Rostand, at the Sarah Bernhardt Theatre (1924).

More demanding and successful was the revival of Edmond Rostand's *La Princesse Lointaine* at the same theatre, which the brothers Isola commissioned after seeing *Aladin* (figs. **80, 81**) in 1929, an enormous production number for which Erté created more than 150 costumes and décors. In *La Princesse Lointaine*, he proved that he could adapt the exuberant decorativeness of his music-hall style to a monumental poetic drama (fig. **82**). The costumes are statuesque and sober, and the total stage pictures achieve a magnificent blend of his oriental stylizations and the concentric motifs of *Art Déco*. Robert de Beauplan in *La Petite Illustration* wrote of 'a manner which bridges the occident and the orient, the Christian middle ages and Byzantium, yet in a style essentially modern.' The press generally compared his efforts favourably with those of Alphonse Mucha for Sarah Bernhardt's original production. *Le Matin* found 'a profound poetry and picturesqueness'; *Paris Soir* praised his 'exquisite taste'; and *Semaine à Paris* described the sets as 'real marvels'.

It was through Weldy that Erté began to be patronized by American producers. Florenz Ziegfeld was the leading exponent of the Broadway parallel of the French revue. His use of the name 'Follies', however, was not in imitation of the French. The idea of a show based on beautiful girls came from his first wife Anna Held, who had herself been a music-hall artiste in France. The title was taken from a newspaper column 'Follies of the Day' and adapted to 'Follies of the Year'. Being superstitious Ziegfeld insisted on exactly thirteen letters in the title, and thus evolved his first show, *Follies of 1907*. It was innocent by modern standards, the only nude appearing in a barrel. But the slogan 'Glorifying the American girl' caught on. Like the French revue, Ziegfeld's shows were originally planned as literally reviews of the foibles of the year. But as in France, the American version soon exchanged comic content for bare flesh and spectacle. This is illustrated in a story of W.C. Fields being auditioned by Ziegfeld. The comedian was worried by the producer's inattention. When Fields came to the end of his routine Ziegfeld asked an assistant how long it took the girls to dress. Seven minutes, he was told. Turning to Fields he ordered, 'Hold your sketch to seven minutes.'

Ziegfeld soon had his imitators—notably George White; there were also Earl Carroll's *Vanities*, Lee and J.J. Schuberts' *Artists and Models* at the Winter Garden, and the *Greenwich Village Follies*. Erté's work eventually appeared in all of these. The producers came to Paris regularly in search of new talent, both in performers and designers. Ziegfeld commissioned an Erté number *L'Or* after seeing it in Paris and put it into his *Follies* of 1923

83 'The Golden Calf', 1924

84 'Vestale', 1924

85 'Aphrodite', 1924

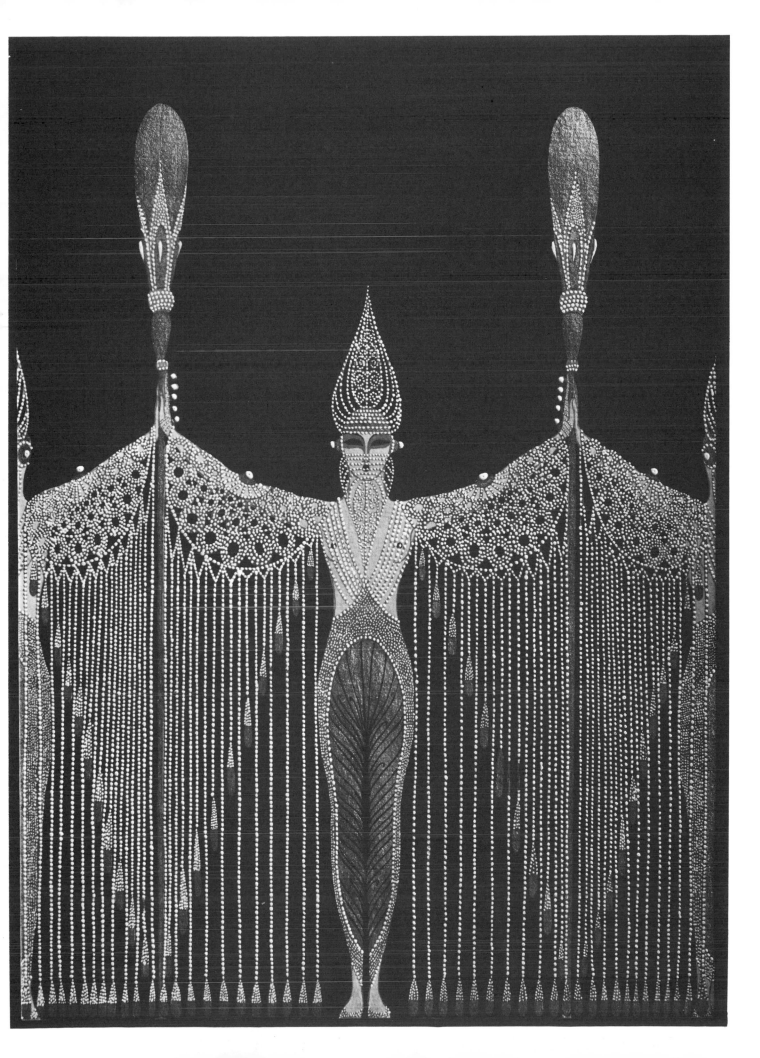

87 'Lotus', 1922

88 The Mother of Pearl Ballet, 1922

89 'The Kiss of the Courtesan', 1921

90 'The Maternal Kiss', 1921

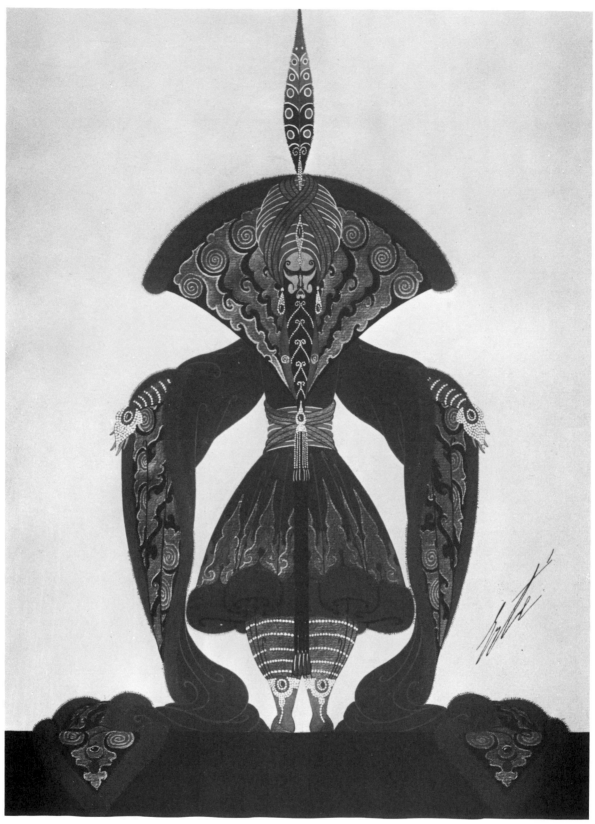

92 The Sultan, *Aladin,* 1929

or 1924. (When Erté was in New York in 1925 the number was being revived.) Similarly, the Schubert brothers bought for the Winter Garden *La Femme et le Diable* (figs. 93, 94, 95), a huge production number first seen at the Apollo Theatre, Paris.

When he came to Paris in 1922, George White saw Erté's *Les Mers* at the Ambassadeurs. He ordered it from Weldy who asked Erté to come to Paris to meet the American producer. This was the beginning of a close and amicable association. Erté's first contributions to the *Scandals* were rapturously received. *The New York Bulletin* wrote: 'The production represents the last word in costume designing and color blending, elaborate curtains and lighting effects. The introduction of the famous Erté costumes, without limit in originality and variety, caused gasps of wonderment from the first night audience.' The *New York Daily Mirror* confirmed 'that the costumes are little short of breathtaking in their grandeur. There was the lace curtain, the silver curtain, the gold curtain, and by way of a five-star climax, the diamond curtain.'

In the words of the obituary in the *New York Times* (12 October 1968), George White's shows were 'innocently sexy revues that captured the giddy 'twenties.' In addition to girls and spectacles the *Scandals* were noted for George Gershwin's music and the dancing—George White's own speciality. Born Weitz in New York's East side in 1890, he started as a song and dance man, and appeared in the *Ziegfeld Follies* of 1915. He was responsible for popularizing such dances as the Turkey Trot, the Charleston (fig. 98) and the Black Bottom (fig. 99), the latter said to have been invented by himself. White staged his first show in 1921 and mounted, in all, thirteen editions of the famous *George White's Scandals*. His early stars included W.C.Fields, Harry Richman, Rudy Vallee, Moran and Mack; later there were Dolores Costello, Helen Morgan, Alice Faye, Ethel Merman, Kate Smith, Eleanor Powell and Ann Miller.

The last *Scandals* was staged in 1939; White had already suffered a series of bankruptcies, due to his lavish spending and a predilection for horseracing. In New York, and indeed everywhere else, the costly spectacular revue died with the war.

Erté's last show for George White was in 1929 (almost the same year as the end of his contract with the Folies-Bergère), at the time of the economic collapse. They remained on good terms; White asked him to design his revue at the 1936 San Francisco World's Fair, which seems to have set a precedent since Erté later worked on *Wonder World* for the New York World's Fair in 1964, and *Flying Colours* at Expo 67, Montreal, which provided a reunion with Maurice Chevalier, with whom he first worked at the Ba-ta-Clan half a century previously.

Erté's theatrical work eventually took the form of colourful pageants at which the only singing or speaking was in the form of a commentary on the personages or the subjects depicted. These might be in the form of oriental pantomimes, characters from myth or history, as in *Les Idoles*, or fantastic inventions based on jewels, perfumes, flowers, rivers, seas, countries and the like. For these numbers Erté began to invent completely new forms of presentation. From harmonious groups of costumes when an historical personage or an emblem would appear with attendants, he elaborated

96 'The Arctic Sea', 1925

94 & 95 La Bergere de France and her Page, 1923

97 Spirals costume, 1925

98 'Charleston', 1925

99 'Black Bottom', 1925

100 'The Handbag', 1926

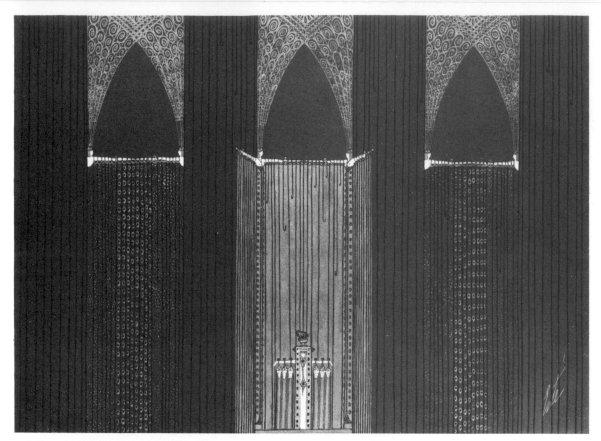

101 Curtain for *The Golden Fables*, 1926

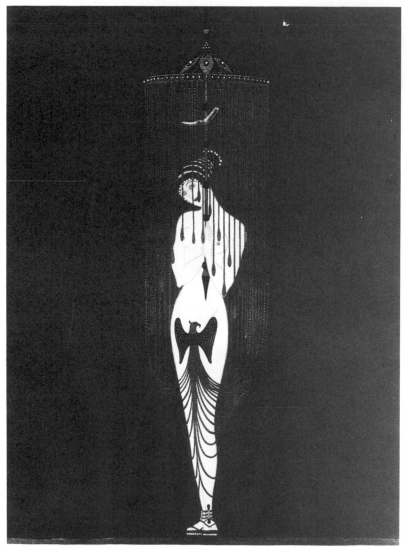

102 Costume for *The Golden Fables*, 1926

103 Slave Costume, 1921

104 'Moods', 1926

105 'The Guadalquivir', *The Rivers*, 1923

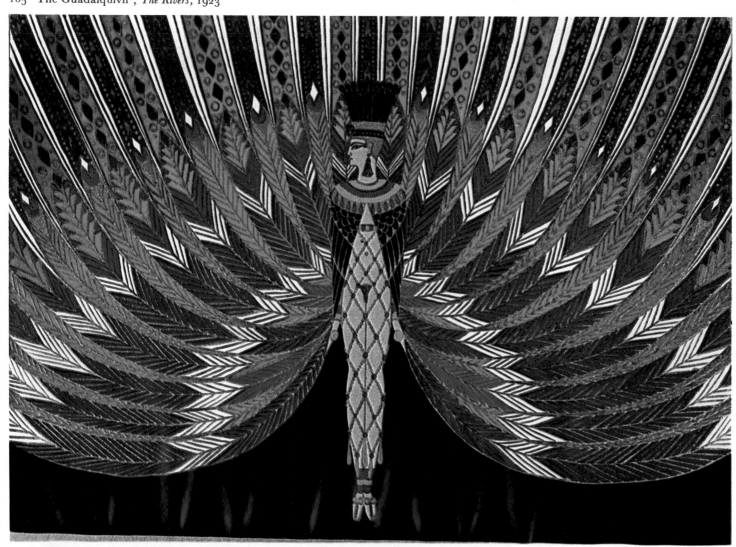

106 'The Nile', 1925

107 'Silk', 1927

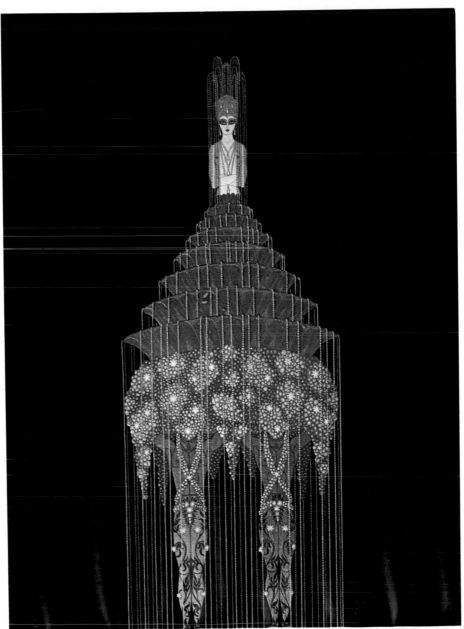

108 'Perfumes', 1927

109 Setting for a Fancy Dress Ball, for the film *Restless Sex*, 1919

110 'Zeus' from the film *Restless Sex*, 1919

111 Costume for Ganna Walska for *Zaza*, 1920

112 *Les Mamelles de Tirésias*, 1947

113 Perpetuum Mobile, 1961

114 Poster for Theodore Kosloff's Ballet School, Hollywood

costumes collectifs, gigantic single garments worn by a group of figures representing a single theme. There is an interesting prototype in *The Kiss of Fire* for *Les Baisers* (1921), when the embracing couple wear what is in fact a single, enveloping costume (fig. 116). Among the finest examples done for the Folies-Bergère and George White are *Rivers* (figs. 105, 106) and *The Seas*. Of the latter a photograph taken at the *Scandals* in 1923 shows the principal performer in the centre of the stage whilst three unseen assistants, wearing the enormous costume over their heads and bodies, help simulate the movement of water. Perhaps the most beautiful collective design is *Silk* (fig. 107) (now in the Victoria and Albert Museum, London).

A second development from this idea was even more spectacular. Erté produced a series of curtains partly made up of live bodies; the earliest recorded example is for *Conte Hindou* (figs. 68, 76). On this occasion ten black slaves, five to a curtain, walked on in profile, each with his head and a shoulder and arm through one aperture, and a leg through another. The curtains were in brilliant red with the visible parts of the bodies framed in elaborate blue and silver embroidery—the colours brilliantly contrasting with the black figures. From this relatively simple device Erté produced in 1924 his most amazing curtain, for an African ballet presented by George White. At the end of the scene what appeared to be live curtains of feathers moved together on the stage. They were made of hundreds of huge black and white plumes, rising to the entire height of the proscenium arch, attached to the wigs and shoulders of two lines of Negresses walking in profile. Each girl rested one arm on the shoulder in front of her, thus enabling long fringes of beads to form part of the total design. The original drawing (fig. 117) is appropriately in the Museum of Modern Art in New York. The following year Erté presented George White with another variation, involving a mechanism used at the Folies-Bergère—girls suspended from the top of the stage, usually as the torsos for outsize crinolines, or living statues on fountains and other architectural structures (fig. 108). The *Diamond Curtain* (fig. 118) filled an alcove at the rear of the stage. Three girls were suspended, the central one above, the others either side, their feet resting on the platform. These two appear to be standing on multiple strands of diamonds which then rise in diagonal lines, whilst others descend from the girl acting as the central pivot.

The distinguishing feature of Erté's work for George White, however, is not to be found in the repetition of oriental themes and spectacular ensembles, which either in fact or by inspiration originated from Paris. (On rare occasions the exchange was reversed; an amusing costume for two girl singers for George White was later adopted by the Dolly Sisters at the Casino de Paris (fig. 152).) What are distinctive are the modern, jazzy numbers, more in the tradition of the American musical stage. I have already referred to costumes for the Charleston and the Black Bottom, and the Negro curtain for the African Ballet. Erté also designed *Indian Dagger Dance* (fig. 120), borrowing from Red Indian and South American motifs, which he was later to use in London and elsewhere. He produced designs for the famous number *The Birth of the Blues* and a series of curtains for Victor Herbert songs. Discussing *On the Crest of a Wave*, sung by Harry Richman, *Women's Wear Daily* (3 July 1928) stated: 'The costumes of the most

115 'Diamond and Attendants', 1926

116 'The Kiss of Fire', 1921

117 Curtain for an African Ballet, 1924

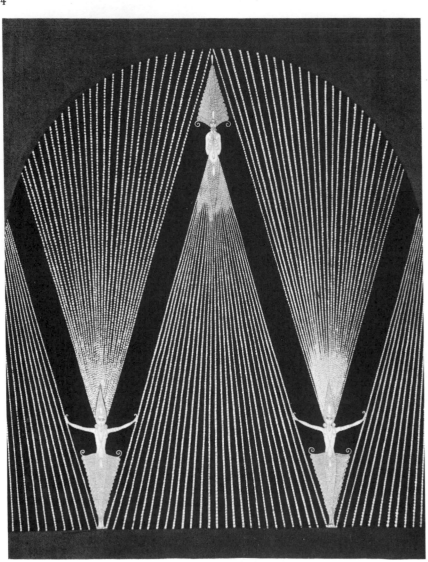

118 Diamond curtain for *The Treasures*, 1925

119 **One of the figures in the African Ballet curtain, 1924** (opposite)

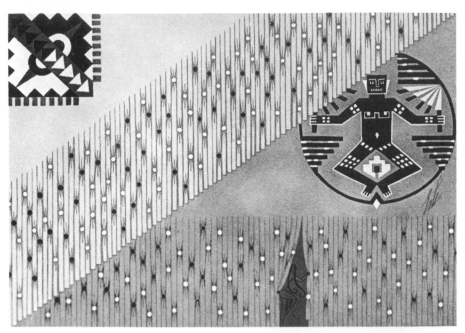

120 Indian Dagger Dance curtain, 1928

121 Opening Curtain for *Manhattan Mary*, 1927

122 Snakeskin Curtain for *Manhattan Mary*, 1927

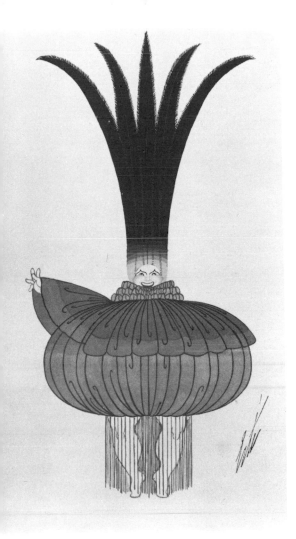

123 Onion costume for a Vegetable Ballet, 1926

124 Potato costume, 1926

elaborate tableaux are sumptuously jeweled and resplendent. There was immediate applause for the rhythmic raising of the water-blue curtains glistened with a crystal sheen.'

Erté's finest Broadway show was probably the musical comedy *Manhattan Mary*, which George White presented at the Majestic Theatre in 1927, starring Ed Wynn. Able to co-ordinate the whole production, he produced a series of delightful costumes (fig. 153) and among the curtains two outstanding designs— one based on the Manhattan sky line (fig. 121) and the other entirely made in snake-skin (fig. 122). One other George White item should be mentioned, the deliciously witty *Vegetable Ballet* (figs. 123, 124).

It is difficult, even when studying the original designs, to imagine the effect of their materialization at the Folies-Bergère or on Broadway. Those of us who for reasons of age or geography could not have seen these shows, must be grateful to Georges Barbier who wrote this evocative description for the catalogues of Erté's exhibitions in Paris and New York in 1929:

> I appreciate him above all when on the stage of the music-hall he brings out of the earth a net-work of diamonds throbbing on nude bodies, when he unfurls curtains embroidered with fantastic birds, or when again he raises curtains woven with ostrich feathers and heavy with fur, or harems afire, or on Eastern cities built of snow, of nacre or metal. It is no easy task to wrench the blasé spectator from his seat in the stalls or to carry him away on the magic carpet to a world of splendour to the accompaniment of stormy music that rises to the head like a strong beverage. The velvet curtain rises slowly, one might even say reluctantly, on the large golden staircase down which descend beautiful snowy women. Their bodies, almost immaterial, are so perfect that all carnal desire is absent before these virginal forms, covered with the pollen of cosmetics, so fragile beneath their towering crowns, and headdresses and accompanied by a cortege of winding sheeny (*sic*) robes resembling dragons held in leash.

CHAPTER 6
HOLLYWOOD: A FRUSTRATING EPISODE

Erté was asked to design for films at almost the same time as Poiret's two other protegés, Iribe and Lepape, and shortly before the third great French illustrator of the period, Georges Barbier.

In the early days of the movies it was usually the director who determined and even designed the décor. D.W.Griffith and Erich von Stroheim, for instance, were totally responsible for the visual aspect of their films. When it came to contemporary clothes it was often left to the actresses to choose. According to Jacques Manuel writing in *La Revue du Cinéma* (Autumn 1949), the first specially created modern film costume was worn by Pearl White in *The Mysteries of New York* (1916)—a black suit with a white blouse and loose tie, plus a velour beret, which virtually became the uniform of New York typists. The designer, who was also the director, was a Frenchman Louis Gasnier. In 1918 Lepape designed costumes for a French film *Phantasmes*, and in the same year Iribe was invited to Hollywood by Cecil B.DeMille to work on *Male and Female* (released 1919) based on James Barrie's play *The Admirable Crichton*. It starred Gloria Swanson and should also be remembered for a Babylonian flashback in which the young Martha Graham performed a lascivious dance. In Paris, Barbier designed the costumes for Rudolph Valentino's film *Monsieur Beaucaire* (1924).

Among the pioneers in Hollywood at this time was Wilfred Buckland, a distinguished theatre-designer, who went into movies in 1914 and also worked for DeMille. The greatest art achievement of the silent era was the gigantic sets for Griffith's *Intolerance*, which in some respects have never been surpassed. William Randolph Hearst, who, as we shall see, played a leading role in Erté's brief film career, set new standards by employing Joseph Urban, the famous Viennese designer of the Ziegfeld Follies.

It was Cecil B.DeMille who first approached Erté. The introduction was made by the wife of Theodore Kosloff, whom Erté had met in the South of France. Kosloff, a fellow-Russian and a former ballet dancer, appeared in a Hollywood movie as early as 1917, *The Woman God Forgot* with Geraldine Farrar and Wallace Reid. He usually played oriental or exotic roles and starred with Gloria Swanson, Bebe Daniels, Betty Compson and Anna Q. Nilsson, mostly in films made by DeMille. In Hollywood Kosloff also ran a school of dance, for which Erté designed a magnificent poster (fig. 114).

Mr DeMille invited Erté to work on a proposed film entitled *The Prodigal Son*. (I can trace no record of his having made it.) When news of this offer reached the ears of William Randolph Hearst, the owner of *Harper's Bazar*, to whom Erté was under contract, the publisher persuaded the artist to turn it down in favour of a contract with Hearst's own Cosmopolitan Films, then in production at Sulzer's Harlem River Park Casino, New York.

Hearst entered the film industry in 1913 with a newsreel, Hearst-Selig Weekly. In association with Pathé-Frères he pioneered the melodrama-serial, including the famous *Perils of Pauline* with Pearl White, followed by *The Exploits of Elaine*, *Seven Pearls* and *Patria*. Not only were they directed and partly written by Hearst, he invented simultaneous serialization on screen and newsprint. In 1917 Hearst met Marion Davies who was a chorus girl in the *Ziegfeld Follies* of that year—in good company with Billie Dove, Mae Murray, Dorothy Mackail, and Will Rogers and Eddie Cantor, all of whom were to achieve fame in Hollywood. Hearst was thirty-five years older than Miss Davies, but it was to be one of the great love affairs of the century, ending only in his death in 1951. 'It was Hearst's considered intention to make Miss Davies the greatest screen star in the nation,' writes his biographer W.A.Swanberg. Among the methods he used was one which had succeeded in his newspaper empire—always to employ the best. 'He was a crank on authenticity in costumes and sets,' Mr Swanberg tells us. W.R. Werner, a former Cosmopolitan publicity man, writing in *The New Yorker* (14 September 1940) further explains: 'Mr Hearst loved to see Miss Davies dress in beautiful clothes, so most of her pictures used to have a fairytale interlude.' To achieve this end Hearst employed Joseph Urban, not only to design the movies but to redesign the cinemas where the premières were held, usually in the period style of the films. The cost was prodigious. No wonder that when someone remarked to Hearst, 'There's money in movies,' he answered, 'Yes—mine!'

Another notable feature of Cosmopolitan Films was Hearst's jealous eye on Miss Davies' leading men. Dick Powell once related how nerve-racking such an experience could be, in view of Hearst's immense wealth and power and the vulnerability of a struggling young actor.

Given Hearst's paranoic possessiveness towards his staff, and his anxiety to surround Marion Davies with the finest talent money could buy, it is not surprising that he should forestall Cecil B.DeMille's initiative to employ an artist made famous through the pages of *Harper's Bazar*. Nor is it surprising, in view of his predilection for 'fairy-tale interludes', that he should commission Erté in 1919 to work on a sequence called *Bal des Arts*. Erté himself had forgotten whether it was destined for a particular film until *Harper's Bazar* for April 1920 revealed two pages of reproductions headed 'The Egyptian Influence in Dress Makes Erté's Designs for the *Restless Sex* most interesting'. A caption refers to a forthcoming 'film version of Robert W.Chambers' *Restless Sex*'. It was in fact released in December 1920, starring Marion Davies and directed by Robert Z.Leonard, who married Mae Murray and later directed a number of films Erté worked on in Hollywood in 1925.

Erté's designs represent, in my view, one of his finest achievements. The difference between them and the work done in Hollywood in 1925 is striking and significant. *Bal des Arts* was the most important commission for the then twenty-seven-year-old artist. He had not yet begun the series of lavish spectacles for the Folies-Bergère, nor the Broadway revues.

Bal des Arts represents an important stage in his career. It is the apotheosis of his oriental style. The influence of Russian theatrical design, with its strong Eastern flavour, has already been noted. In this genre *Bal des Arts* is his masterpiece. The ballroom setting is like a vast Babylonian hanging-garden, which connoisseurs of early cinematic architecture will not fail to recognize (fig. **109**). The style was a bridge between *Art Nouveau* and the emergent *Art Déco* of the 'twenties. For the costumes Erté ranged through Greek mythology, Egyptian idolatry, Indian iconography and all manner of exotica to create an anthology of magnificent figures. The detail of the robes is astonishing in inventiveness, precision, erotic suggestion and playful humour. They are not merely designs for dresses; the figures are performers in movement or repose, full of energy, grace or statuesque dignity; without doubt among the finest costume designs of the century (figs. **110**, 125, 126, **154**).

By 1925, when Erté was again called on by the cinema, he enjoyed greater fame in the United States. In the interval he had created a splendid series of costumes for the opera singer Ganna Walska and numerous spectacles for the French music-hall. In 1922 he started a long association with George White's *Scandals* and, of course, he continued his monthly contributions to *Harper's Bazar*. He had also held his first exhibition at the Knoedler Gallery on Fifth Avenue, New York, in 1920.

It is almost certainly due to William Randolph Hearst that Erté eventually visited Hollywood in 1925. A year previously the Metro-Goldwyn-Mayer Corporation was formed and Louis B. Mayer (1885–1957) became Vice President in charge of production. Mayer had been born in Russia and brought as a child to Nova Scotia, where his father worked as a junk dealer. At the age of twenty-two he bought his first cinema in Haverhill, Massachusetts, and later obtained the local distributing rights of *The Birth of a Nation*. He started production in Hollywood in 1918. A close friend and admirer of William Randolph Hearst, he offered Cosmopolitan Films an independent base in the new MGM Culver City studio, with an eye no doubt on the publicity potential of the vast Hearst press. It was at this time that Hearst began to build his great castle San Simeon with its '240,000 acre front yard' and priceless art treasures. For Marion Davies he put up a fourteen-room dressing-room on the MGM lot which Lady Diana Duff Cooper found to be 'as big as a church'; but that was nothing compared to Miss Davies' 'beach-cottage' with ninety rooms, two swimming pools, three dining-rooms (one with a genuine 14-carat gold ceiling) and a private theatre.

When in 1924 Mayer announced among his first productions a film to be entitled *Paris*, the story of a famous French couturier, it seems not unlikely that Hearst recommended his protégé Erté, whom he considered a great dress-designer and who, since Cosmopolitan's 1919 commission, had also proved himself a brilliant stage-designer. This theory is strengthened by the fact that under his Hollywood contract Erté could not undertake any work outside the MGM studio, except for Hearst's *Harper's Bazar*.

At the time Erté was again living near Paris. In 1923 he had taken a house in Sèvres, which Georges Barbier, writing in the *Gazette du Bon Ton* for April 1924, described as follows:

A charming house in the environs of Paris . . . the interior is full of spells.

125 'Sultan', 1919

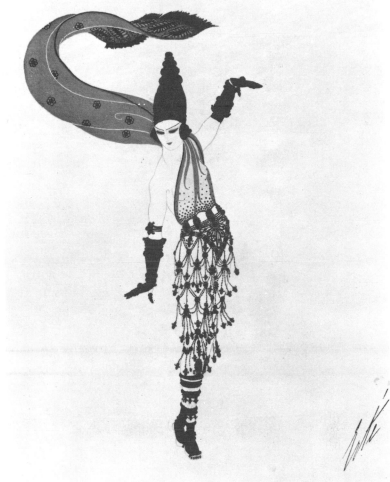

126 'Yacodhara', 1919

127 Erté in his studio at Sèvres, 1924

There are wooden walls and floors of mosaic and harmonies of grey, the grey of steel and the grey of Siamese cats. On the grey carpets grey cushions are scattered. The walls are covered with curtains, decorated with monograms, from which hang black symmetrical tassels. If you pull the cords the curtains part, revealing hundreds of designs of the theatre. One thinks of the glass cases of entomologists where butterflies display their brilliance . . . the fantasy of the decorator helps this illusion; here, personified, is ivory, ebony, mother-of-pearl, rubies and pearls, gigantic tiaras, interminable sleeves worn by slaves, coats which glisten like snow embraced by declining sun. The adornments made with diamonds, feathers or fur are not intended to cover nudity, but to deliciously intensify it, to encase or frame it, like a chosen gem. This is the house of the designer Erté, one of the artists whose inventiveness has greatly enriched the modern theatre. He has an oriental sense of colour and imagination which leaves his imitators far behind. As one composes a bouquet of flowers, so Erté showed me his innumerable designs. His technique and the impeccable finish of his gouaches made me think of the labour of young white monks who work in the radiance of their cells. . . . I admired also the studies executed for a piece by Shakespeare . . . but I prefer the infinite fairy-like possibilities of revue, when he personified a lotus, or moonbeam, when he makes a jet of water dance or turn in the kaleidoscope of his fantasy. . . .

Mr Mayer's representative who called on Erté at Sèvres was equally impressed; so much so that the photographers snapped the artist and the studio from every angle and when he arrived in Culver City, some months later, he was amazed to find his studio recreated in every detail (fig. 129).

Erté was put under contract by Louis B. Mayer to design the film *Paris*. On 25 February 1925, accompanied by his cousin Prince Nicholas Ourousoff, he arrived in New York in the French liner *France*. The New York newspapers gave him a rousing welcome. 'Erté arrives in New York to create MGM Fashions.' Already famous in the United States for his *Harper's Bazar* covers and Broadway revues, in the words of a reporter echoing Ziegfeld's slogan, Erté was engaged to 'Glorify the American girl on the silver screen'. He had clearly been well rehearsed and declared, 'The American woman is the best dressed of all women'—an opinion he was to retract on leaving the United States before the end of the year.

In inviting Erté to Hollywood Louis B. Mayer wanted to bring a new elegance to film décor. 'Romain de Tirtoff Erté,' stated the *New York American*, 'youngest and leading costume-designer of Europe, whose creations have brought him international fame, arrived yesterday. . . . He will go immediately to California to design costumes for the film actresses of Metro-Goldwyn-Mayer Pictures Productions.' 'Erté's advent into motion pictures,' added *The Morning Telegraph*, 'is considered of special significance to the film industry as it is the first notable recognition paid to the importance of the costuming phase in motion picture production.'

In New York the publicity campaign included a tour of MGM movie theatres. On Erté's arrival the orchestras struck up the Imperial Russian National Anthem—eight years after the revolution! He was referred to variously as prince, duke or count. Before moving to California, Erté held an exhibition at the Madison Gallery, New York. On March 12 William B.M'Cormick reviewed the exhibition in the *New York American*, under the headline: 'Erté Exhibition is a Wow.' It is interesting that this notice treats Erté's work with the same enthusiasm, in some cases in virtually the same terms as the critics who saw his work for the first time in the New York and London 'revivals' of 1967. Mr M'Cormick urged 'every art, theatre, ballet and opera lover to go and see for the delight they will take in Tirtoff-Erté's exquisite creations . . . these watercolors are markedly brilliant as drawings, whilst his color is marvellous both as to range and beauty, the only thing comparable to it I know being that of the finest Persian miniatures'.

In New York Erté earned notoriety for his views on men's clothes. The subject pursued him during his whole stay in the United States, either a cleverly manipulated publicity stunt or, as seems likely, a genuinely prophetic intuition. Almost immediately on his arrival in New York, *The Sun* published his views on male attire:

At his suite in the Ritz-Carlton, Mr Erté told a representative of *The Sun* that men were a blot on the social scene. 'Their clothes are never harmonious,' continued the designer; 'they ruin the ensemble.' Mr Erté himself was an extremely harmonious picture at the moment. He was wearing a boudoir costume of grey crêpe de chine trousers and blouse with narrow rose-coloured borders, over which was a dressing gown of grey and fuschia printed crêpe. Mr Erté has come here to design costumes for the feminine stars of the Metro Goldwyn Corporation and will go to California for that purpose. But this is only the commercial object of his visit. In one of his fifteen trunks he has brought the concrete expression of his deeper motive. It is the evening suit of brownish violet which he hopes will serve as a suggestion to other men that they can wear something new in evening clothes and still live.

En route to Hollywood the cousins were photographed in Chicago as 'Apostles of Violet Dress Suits'. A cartoon in the *Los Angeles Examiner*, depicting the clothes Erté proposed for men, showed a figure in patterned waistcoat and frock-coat, with a floppy, polka-dot tie, long side-burns and ruffles at the wrist. The caricaturist could hardly have realized that his satire would turn to reality forty years later.

To herald his arrival in Hollywood, Erté's photograph appeared in newspapers surrounded by images of the stars he would dress—Mae Murray, Claire Windsor, Paulette Duval, Eleanor Boardman, Renée Adorée, Norma Shearer, Alice Terry and Blanche Sweet.

On 17 March 1925 Louis B.Mayer officially welcomed his new protégé at a luncheon at the Beverly Hills Hotel. Mayer was one of the great Hollywood originals—a partial model for Scott Fitzgerald's *The Last Tycoon*, just as his friend Hearst inspired Orson Welles' *Citizen Kane*. He remained head of production at MGM until 1951 and in the 'thirties and the 'forties earned the largest salary in the United States. In later life he had a reputation for aggressive ruthlessness. Kevin Brownlow, in *The Parade's Gone By* believes that 'History has shown him to be a childishly melodramatic paranoic'. He was often physically violent; he attacked both

Charlie Chaplin and Erich von Stroheim, and on occasions members of his staff had to drag him off visitors with whom he violently disagreed. In *The Movie Moguls* Phillip French quotes Samuel Goldwyn's comment on Mayer's burial: 'One reason so many people showed up at his funeral was because they wanted to be sure he was dead.' Erté, however, despite his disappointed departure from Hollywood after eight frustrating months, says he always found Mayer courteous and intelligent. On his arrival in Hollywood Mayer presented him the gift of a Packard motor-car; and on his departure a signed photograph bearing the inscription: 'To a great artist and friend with best wishes—Louis B. Mayer Nov. 1925.' Even critics of Louis B. Mayer seem to agree that he had a gift for talent-spotting, the best example being his appreciation of Greta Garbo's unique aura even before she spoke English. The director Clarence Brown regarded him as 'one of the greatest brains in the picture business. He made more stars than the rest of the producers in Hollywood put together. He knew how to handle talent; he knew that to be successful he had to have the most successful people in the business working for him.' It was a business philosophy he shared with his friend Hearst.

Apart from Joseph Urban, Hearst's art director, the other important designer Erté got to know in Hollywood was Adrian who was working on Rudolph Valentino's film *The Eagle*. MGM was still in the throes of the drama of *Ben Hur*. In *The Parade's Gone By*, Kevin Brownlow describes the reshooting of the film after the Italian fiasco the previous year. 'Saturday was a Roman holiday for the film colony. Among the thousands who crammed the Circus Maximus were stars of the magnitude of Douglas Fairbanks and Mary Pickford, Harold Lloyd, Lillian Gish, Colleen Moore, Marion Davies and John Gilbert.' Erté too was among the illustrious audience watching the famous chariot race being filmed. He was called on to contribute to the film when an extra scene was added with Carmel Myers in the part of Iras. A photograph of the original design remains, plus one of Miss Myers in her magnificent robe with Erté (figs. 128, 129).

Apart from this costume, Erté's 1925 film designs are all contemporary in style, notably the architectural and interior settings which represent an unusual departure in his work. For fashion magazines, of course, he had always designed contemporary clothes, occasionally shown in interior settings. The theatre, however, whether music-hall, straight plays, opera or ballet had usually called for imaginative fantasies based on historical and period styles.

In *Harper's Bazar* (June 1925) Erté contributed an article entitled 'Here I am in America':

> I have been asked questions such as one would ask a savage transported in a cage to a civilized country. If you prefer statistics to crossword puzzles I can give some figures which I have been gathering. I had on board the liner, in New York, Chicago and Hollywood, 197 interviews with newspaper correspondents; 152 persons have asked me whether I prefer brunettes to blondes; 182 have asked me about bobbed hair; I heard 89 times the question—Who is the most chic woman?

Later he described his impressions of Hollywood:

128 Costume for Carmel Myers in *Ben Hur*

129 Erté with Carmel Myers in 1925

In the huge studio of Metro-Goldwyn-Mayer in Culver City I saw hundreds of young persons able to work who instead are wandering about looking at the sky or down, waiting for something. And at the same time I meet Queens and Caesars telling me that they work like negroes or beggars, who roll up in Rolls-Royces! I see great palaces built without walls in the back—tiny houses with lakes of crystal hanging in the air . . . stairs leading nowhere.

Erté worked on *The Mystic* starring the British-born actress Aileen Pringle, whose fame was based on her resemblance to Elinor Glyn. Conway Tearle played the male lead and the film was directed by Tod Browning. Erté designed evening dresses and coats and two gypsy costumes which seem to have been inspired by Rudolph Valentino's film *The Sheik*. Photographs of Miss Pringle wearing a black velvet gown with white ermine trimmings provide a rare comparison between the design and the finished costume. These photographs were probably taken when she attended the official opening of Erté's studio (figs. 130–133).

Although contracted for the film *Paris*, it soon became clear that Erté's transportation to Hollywood was at worst a publicity stunt, and at best an attempt to buttress the film capital's pretensions. As Lillian Gish writes about her own entry into the MGM empire in the 'twenties, despite 'the great banners strung across the streets of Culver City . . . I discovered that no preparations had been made for me, no stories (not even ideas), no directors—nothing'.

130 Costume for Aileen Pringle in the film *The Mystic*, 1925

131 Costume for Aileen Pringle, 1925

132 Aileen Pringle wearing Erté's costume

133 Gypsy Costume for Aileen Pringle, 1925

Mayer continued to keep Erté busy. After *The Mystic*, his next assignment was a fashion revue called *Her Day* staged on April 20 by the Friends of the Council of Jewish Women at the Ambassador Hotel, Los Angeles, described in the Los Angeles *Daily Examiner* (14 April 1925) as 'the most dazzling array of costumes ever shown in the United States'. The film stars who appeared in this extravaganza included Norma Shearer, Claire Windsor, Eleanor Boardman, Aileen Pringle, Carmel Myers, Pauline Starke and Paulette Duval. Of Erté's contribution there survive a design for Norma Shearer in a veiled, nun-like concoction (figs. 134, 135) and a charming drawing of a masked costume with tassels worn by Paulette Duval. For *Dance Madness*, directed by Robert Z.Leonard, with Aileen Pringle and Lew Cody, he was asked to devise a Mask Ballet. A newspaper report describes 'a stage in bright vermilion on which a large mask is suspended from the ceiling and back of the eyes a spectacular show is ever passing ever changing' For this film Erté created two of his most characteristic dresses, made entirely of strings of pearls or beads, which swing and sway as the figures Charleston with abandon. There are other designs, all masked—one of a black dress has a long train made entirely of rows of pearls hanging from a low-cut back. A black and white coat has sleeves capped over the hand in the form of adders' heads; from each sleeve two false sleeves hang, in black and white fur. The head is covered by a black helmet down to the tip of the nose. As always with Erté at his best, the design embodies a curious mixture of wit and fantasy, such as the echoes of the adder's head on the hands and helmet (figs. 136, 137).

134 Costume for Norma Shearer in *Her Day*, 1925

135 Norma Shearer wearing Erté's costume

136 Evening coat for Aileen Pringle, 1925

137 Costume for the film *Dance Madness*, 1925

A Little Bit of Broadway was another back-stage drama, for which he designed a splendid cushioned foyer and a Cubist dressing-room, coldly geometric in detail, reminiscent of the Bauhaus or de Stijl (fig. 138). From *Time the Comedian*, again directed by Robert Z.Leonard, two drawings show Erté at his most inventive. A masked male figure in black tights has one hand in the form of an aged face, the other framed by a ruff is a clock face with the centre finger pointing to midnight. The soubrette's costume shows her nude from the navel up, except for crossed straps, the little tutu-skirt formed of panniers of *Art Déco* blossoms. Her head-dress is based on the same design and from the top of her head a balloon on a ribbon is a replica of her cherubic face and flower cap (figs. 139, 140).

Erté found other employment whilst waiting for the script for *Paris*. On

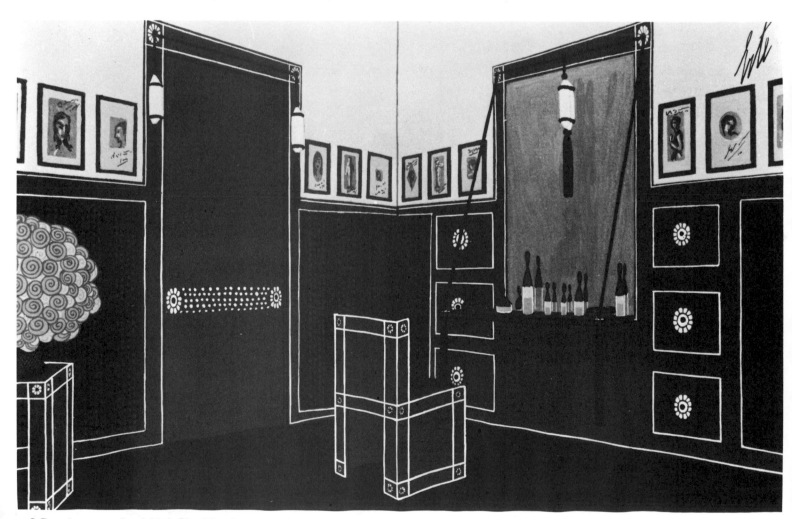

138 Dressing room for *A Little Bit of Broadway*, 1925

4 June 1925 Metro-Goldwyn-Mayer participated in the first Motion Picture Electrical Parade and Pageant at the Coliseum, Los Angeles. Erté, according to newspaper reports, designed 'fantastic and bizarre costumes' representing Hilarity, Comedy, Tragedy and Drama.

The costumes for King Vidor's film *La Bohème* are especially interesting since the leading parts were played by two famous actresses, Lillian Gish and Renée Adorée (partnered by John Gilbert and Edward Everett Horton) and because a disagreement between Miss Gish and Erté hastened his departure from Hollywood, and as I shall relate later, reverberated through the years. Erté's designs for Musette and Mimi are exquisite miniatures and despite Miss Gish's protests some were used in the film— voted as one of the best movies of 1926 (figs. 141, 142).

139 Costume for *Time the Comedian*, 1925

140 Ballet costume for *Time the Comedian*, 1925

141 Costume for Mimi (Lillian Gish) in *La Boheme*, 1925   142 Costume for Musette (Renée Adorée) in *La Bohème*, 1925

On 11 July 1925 the *Exhibitors Herald* included a large advertisement from Metro-Goldwyn-Mayer announcing that 'Erté the World's Foremost Fashion Genius has designed breath-taking styles for Robert Z. Leonard's Production PARIS, with Pauline Starke and Lew Cody'; no such costume designs were ever made. Erté was becoming impatient with Mr Mayer's procrastinations over the script. References to the film were regularly filtered to the press by the studio. One columnist reported seeing drawings for the sets of the picture, which she described as 'something novel in screen settings'. Another announced:

> An amazing ballet entitled The Ballet of the Pearls . . . to be used in the picture *Paris*. The opening curtain of ruby velvet is to be opened by a nude gilded slave who stands in the middle of the stage with cords in his hands. He pulls the cords releasing two counter-balances which descend slowly to the stage and open the curtains. The weights are formed by two beautiful nudes, hanging in the air, whose resemblance to tassels is increased by skirts formed of ropes of pearls hanging from the waist to the feet. They reveal a coffer on the stage, the lock of which is formed of two lovers kissing. At the order of the sultan a dagger slays the lovers and opens the lock, revealing the contents of the casket, beautiful maidens impersonating the various uses of pearls, as rings, necklaces, brooches.

The accuracy of this description can be vouched for by two existent designs (fig. 155). Despite the absence of a script, or even a story line, Erté set about creating a series of elaborate sets in which a complex (if unknown) plot could be played out.

Erté's original six months' contract came to an end with no sign of the film *Paris*. Louis B. Mayer asked him to remain for a further three months and offered to appoint a new director. Edmund Goulding did eventually make a film called *Paris* for MGM, released in June 1926, but what relationship it had to the original idea or whether any of Erté's designs were used, it has been impossible to discover.

Before the end of 1925 Erté 'broke his movie contract in a huff', to quote a contemporary report; 'Hollywood is just waking up to the supreme insult thrown by Romain de Tirtoff-Erté,' continued the newspaper.

The finale to the drama of *Paris* came when a script was eventually produced. For some months Erté had been designing the sets, all in the symmetrical Cubist style of the period. The dining-room is perhaps the finest, literally dripping with leopard skins, draped round the chairs and side tables and on the floor. Equally elaborate is the plan for a huge night-club, with tiny square tables and chairs and geometric light-fittings. There are also drawings for a boudoir, foyers and a salon, a glamorous swimming pool, as well as for the oriental ballet described earlier (figs. 143, 144, 156). When Erté read the script he discovered a story about a Parisian couturier living in the Palais du Louvre. In newspaper interviews he later explained that he 'found the scenario dealing with Paris life simply impossible, ghastly in fact. Neither the director, nor the scenario-writer, not the stars, knew the least bit about life in Paris. It was a huge joke. They were writing about Paris, Texas, and did not know it.' He describes the principal character as 'the couturier Morand living in the ancient palace of the kings of France.

143 Boudoir for *Paris*, 1925

144 Night club set for *Paris*, 1925

138

... With great difficulty I advised them to find another residence for their illegitimate king crowned in organdy.' To his suggestion, the reply was: 'The Louvre's the swellest place in Paris, isn't it—well that's where he lives!' Erté refused to allow his sets to be used and decided to leave Hollywood for good. On his departure Louis B.Mayer publically expressed his regret: 'Erté is a great genius and we believe he has given American films an important artistic contribution. Metro-Goldwyn-Mayer was fortunate in having the benefit of his limited time in this country and we wish him continued success abroad.'

Before leaving, however, Erté made a last contribution to Hollywood, the 'Prologue' at Grauman's Egyptian Theatre on November 15 for the première of King Vidor's famous war film *The Big Parade*, starring John Gilbert and Renée Adorée. Of the costumes representing the allied nations two designs have been traced—Italy, in her national colours, with a headdress representing a lyre and portrait medallions on her train; and Belgium, fittingly tragic, with the huge sword piercing her head to emerge dripping from her stomach (fig. 145).

Having made his decision to leave Hollywood and the United States, Erté left no doubt as to why. 'Paris Artist Sails in Huff'; 'Hollywood Beauties? Bah! They disgust Frenchman'; 'French Fashion Designer Quits Hollywood in Disillusionment'; 'Film Actresses Devoid of Beauty and Wit'; these are a few of the newspaper headlines he left in his trail.

Back in Paris, Erté's break with Hollywood continued to attract attention. On 16 December 1925 the *New York Herald's* Paris edition printed an interview:

American motion pictures are still in the barbarous stage; American producers in Hollywood have not the slightest conception of elegance, beauty or taste; film stars for the most part are illiterate, crotchety, unshapely, even ill formed; scenario writers know nothing of the world outside their small narrow circle—this, in summary, is the confirmed opinion of Count (*sic*) Romain de Tirtoff-Erté . . . who has just returned to Paris after an eight-month stay in the busy cinema capital of the United States.

Erté addressed a letter to *Comœdia*, printed on 24 February 1926, in reply to reports issued in the United States:

Please allow me to explain certain facts which have been misunderstood and to inform you under what circumstances I left Metro-Goldwyn. Contrary to what has been said, I was never the chief of the 'costume department' of this organization. I was employed as a designer of sets and costumes and was entirely independent. A special studio had been built for me where I made my maquettes and a French dressmaker, carefully chosen by me, worked with me on their execution. Consequently nobody was above me for the simple reason that I was alone, and it is not here that we find the cause for my departure. We cannot find it either in my dispute with Lillian Gish. I was to design her costumes for *La Vie Bohème* but I was obliged to abandon it because of her personal conception of the work of Murger and the role of Mimi. For example, she wanted all her

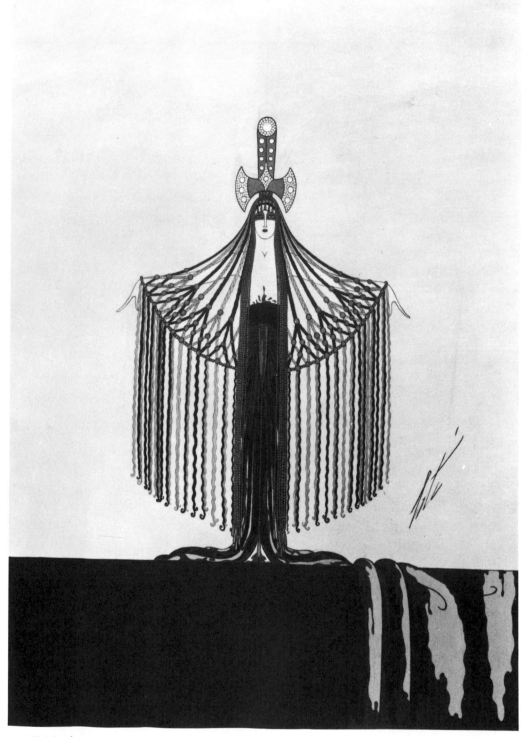

145 '*Belgium*', 1925

costumes, even the poorest, to be made in silk. I now come to why I left Metro-Goldwyn. I had originally been engaged to design costumes and sets for a 'superfilm' called *Paris* which was to be presented as 'Erté's production' and which was so announced before it had been realised. This film which was to illustrate to the American public the life of the French capital turned Paris into a caricature. Paris, the capital of art became simply the capital of fashion and the kingdom of violence. I could not take part in such a betrayal and it was for this reason that I asked for my contract, which had another four months to run, to be cancelled.

Rumbles of Erté's row with Hollywood still echo from the past. In her autobiography, published in 1969, Lillian Gish explains that on finding no concrete plans for her début with Metro-Goldwyn-Mayer, she herself suggested the film *La Bohème* based on Murger's famous story. She continues:

When I heard that Erté, the top designer of the time, had been brought over from Paris to do the costumes, I was pleased. I thought he would know just how Mimi should look. But at the first fitting I found that all the costumes looked like brand new dresses. I explained that Mimi was being put out of her attic because she could not pay the rent. 'Don't you know that this is made of calico that costs only five shillings a yard?' he said, pointing to one dress. 'Yes, but on the screen it would look like a nice new dress,' I objected. 'Old worn silk would look poorer and much better. This stiff material won't act.' He became angry with me and refused to co-operate, so I went to our wardrobe mistress Madame Coulter with reproductions of paintings, and we re-designed Mimi's clothes. I tried without success to persuade Renée Adorée to do the same.

Of course Miss Gish is mistaken in assuming that he was brought to Hollywood to design her film. He recalls their quarrel, based, he says, on Miss Gish's refusal to wear anything except silk, because of her tender skin. In fact the dresses were not made from calico but wool, which photogenically would have given both a soft and simple effect. As Miss Gish indicates, her co-star did not agree with her, so that in the film Renée Adorée's costumes for Musette were all as designed by Erté.

146 Costume for the *Bal Tabarin*, c. 1936   147 Costume for Cecile Sorel as Madame du Barry, 1935

CHAPTER 7
NEW TECHNIQUES

The 'thirties saw many changes in Erté's personal life, as well as in fashion, journalism and the theatre—the areas in which he had already won fame.

When he left Monte Carlo for Sèvres in 1923 he arranged for his parents to remain at the Villa Excelsior. His father died in 1928 and a year later his mother moved to Paris. She died at the age of eighty-four in 1948. A great loss, both personally and to the business side of his career, was the tragic death of Prince Nicholas in the mid-'thirties as a result of a gardening accident. Soon after this Erté moved to Auteuil and then in 1935 to the apartment overlooking the Bois de Boulogne where he still lives.

As I have explained, his work with the Folies-Bergère and George White came to an end with the economic depression of 1929–30. In 1933 he started a long association with Pierre Sandrini at the Bal Tabarin, which only ended with the producer's death in 1952. The son of the prima ballerina Emma Sandrini, his shows, more modest than the earlier revues, introduced ballet sequences and speciality acts in place of well-known stars. Erté's contribution was in the form of elegant and amusing costumes which formed spectacular tableaux, not the exotic or oriental extravaganzas of former years (fig. 146).

During this period, and indeed after 1952, Erté continued to work for other French theatres, notably the Châtelet, the Marigny and the ABC where Cecile Sorel made her music-hall début (fig. 147). He has designed a number of dramatic productions, among them Daudet's *Sappho* at the Sarah Bernhardt Theatre in 1934 and *Phèdre* by Racine at the Théâtre du Vieux Colombier in 1960. He continued to design for theatres abroad—the Calderón and Cómico in Barcelona, the Scala Theatre, Berlin, the Quattro Fontane in Rome. In North America, apart from the contributions I have mentioned to international exhibitions, New York saw his work at the Latin Quarter in 1964–65.

Through Weldy occasional items by Erté had appeared in English shows but it was not until 1937 that London audiences were able to judge his full talents. Cecil Landeau, part-author and director of a revue called *It's in the Bag*, sought him out via Weldy. The result (figs. 148, 149), at the Saville Theatre, was immensely successful. The *Daily Telegraph* said of the show: 'Especially does it appeal to and satisfy the eye,' and the *News Chronicle* referred to 'brilliant costumes and settings'. 'The real hero of the evening,' concluded the critic of the *Evening News*, 'is a mysterious Erté who has done

148 Aztec Ballet Costume, 1937

149 Set for *It's in the Bag*, 1937

150 'Samson and Delilah', 1926

151 'The Golden Calf', 1926

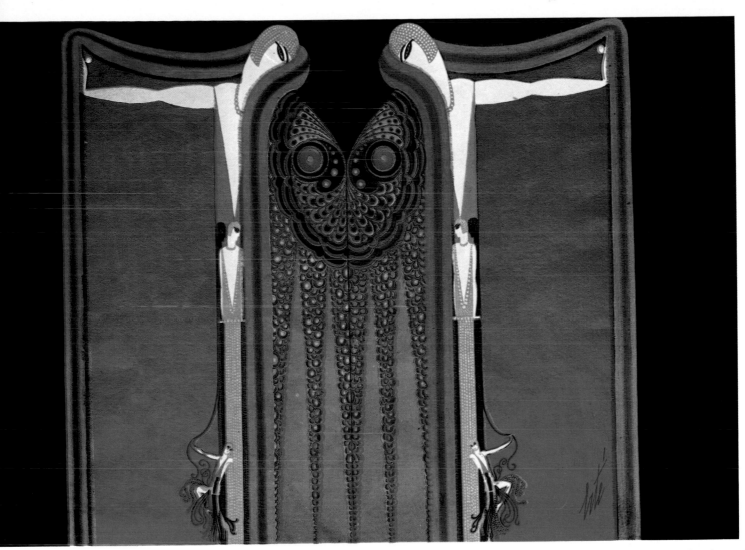

152 The *Two Sisters Curtain*, 1926

153 Costume for *Manhattan Mary*, 1927

154 'Hera' in *Restless Sex*, 1919

155 Setting for an oriental ballet in the film *Paris*, 1925

156 Dining Room for *Paris,* 1925

157 Costume for Mary Garden in the opera *L'Amore dei Tre Re,* 1926

all the scenery and costumes. He, or she, is a bit of a genius; not even in Mr Cochran's great days have I ever seen a show more continuously beautiful to the eye.' The *Sunday Times* felt that as a 'great deal of importance is being attached to the décor', they should explain that 'Erté is a Russian artist . . . living in Paris, and that although his work is unknown in London, he has been associated with three big Broadway shows'.

The following year he worked with George Black at the Palladium and London Hippodrome, and in 1946 with Robert Nesbitt at the Coliseum. London also saw his designs for the French revue *La Plume de Ma Tante* before it was taken to New York in 1958. His last show in London was at the Victoria Palace in 1960.

There are distinct changes in this period. No longer could he depend on lavish materials, costly mechanical aids, nor, for that matter, the same standards of dressmaking and decoration. There emerged a broader style. Whilst vestiges of oriental and historical preoccupations remain, it is noteworthy that instead of the Arabian Nights there are other forms of exotica— South Sea islands, Bali, Mexico. A link with an earlier manner is *Au Temps des Merveilleuses* (fig. 158) for the Théâtre du Châtelet in 1934. The elegant 'directoire' gowns were decorated with embroideries, jewels and plumes, but less ornate and costly than previously. The return to a longer, more feminine line in fashion brought out the elegance of his early drawings. This is also evident in his work for the Bal Tabarin in the 'thirties. One of his most charming and amusing series of costumes was made for *London Symphony* at the London Palladium in 1938 (figs. 159, 160). Four sets of show-girls, *Symphonies* in White, Black, Grey and Brown, were dressed in slinky gowns heavily trimmed in furs of the appropriate colours. His characteristic wit can be seen in a 1945 Bal Tabarin number, when the girls represented musical terms (fig. 161). Designs for the 1945 show at the Calderón Theatre, Barcelona, are notable for bold, simple shapes and strong primary colours (fig. 162)—similar to his operatic work of this period.

Perhaps the most notable feature of Erté's career after the Second World War was his involvement with opera and ballet. Given his musical background, his childhood passion for opera and ballet at the Maryinsky Theatre, his devotion to the *Ballets Russes*, it may seem strange that he avoided these theatrical forms for so long. It was largely circumstantial that in the 'twenties and 'thirties other commitments did not permit him to undertake any large-scale productions. Also, at that time opera houses did not offer so many opportunities for the lavish productions we are now accustomed to. Until comparatively recently leading singers commissioned costumes which accompanied them on their operatic rounds. (I even recall two such cases recently at Covent Garden. The Russian soprano Galina Visnevskaya brought her own bright red dress for *Aida* to London, overcoming objections by the pronouncement that it was the colour of the Soviet flag. Then in 1969 the American singer Jess Thomas wore his own dashing silver 'Batman's' suit in a new production of *Die Meistersinger von Nurnberg*.)

It was as a designer of individual costumes that Erté first worked in opera and ballet. In 1920 he received a visit in Monte Carlo from Ganna Walska, a strikingly beautiful woman of Polish origin, who a few years earlier had appeared in revue at the Théâtre des Capucines in Paris. Since then she

158 Directoire costume, 1934

159 'Symphony in Black', 1938

160 'Symphony in Grey', 1938

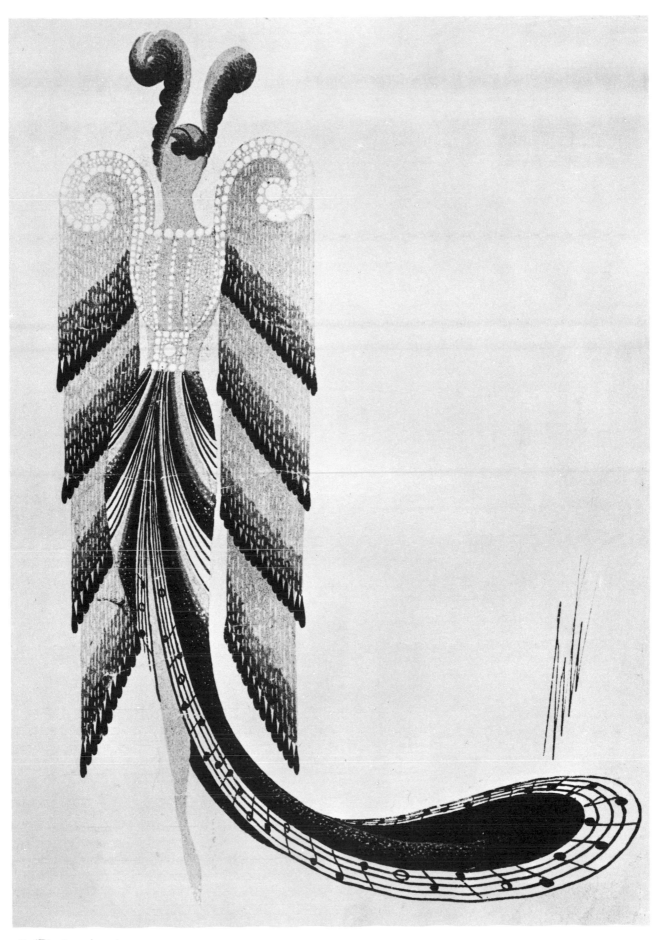

161 'The Symphony', 1945

162 'Amazon', 1945

163 Costume for Ganna Walska for *Rigoletto*, 1920

had developed pretentions to the operatic stage and with her marriage to the millionaire sportsman and carpet king Alexander Smith Cochrane, was planning to appear at the Chicago Opera House. Ronald Davis, the author of *Opera in Chicago*, says of Madame Walska that her 'main ability seems to have been an extraordinary talent for collecting wealthy husbands'. Her ambitions for Chicago materialized through the intervention of Harold F.McCormick, head of the International Harvester Company and one of the main backers of opera in the city. A few years later he divorced his wife to marry Ganna Walska. Her call on Erté was to commission a series of lavish costumes for the principal soprano roles, in which she hoped to appear in Chicago, as well as concert gowns, including one for Beethoven's Ninth Symphony. The only one she ever came near to wearing in Chicago was a dress for Leoncavallo's *Zaza* (fig. 111). Her début was due to take place on 21 December 1920 but during the final rehearsals she lost her temper after the producer continuously asked her to sing louder, and walked out of the opera house.

This lack of volume bedevilled her career. Erté recalls her 1921 début in Paris, in *Rigoletto*, wearing his costumes (fig. 163). Together with other friends, including Prince Yousoupoff, supposedly the assassin of Rasputin, who was Erté's neighbour at Boulogne-sur-Seine, he was invited to the opera and the celebration supper afterwards. 'But,' she added to Erté, 'don't come if it's not a success.' He remembers the performance as a splendid social occasion, the women aglitter in tiaras and magnificent jewels. The first act started well, with an excellent tenor and baritone. For *Caro Nome*, Madame Walska wore a beautiful white gown and high Venetian sandals. The orchestra played but no sound was heard from the singer. Her mouth was certainly wide open, but apparently nerves had affected her larynx. She darted from one side of the stage to the other, and then, suddenly, sound emerged—'As though someone had stepped on the tail of a cat'—recalls Erté. The audience tried in vain to hide their amused embarrassment. In the second act she massaged her stomach in a comforting gesture, but in the great quartet the accompanying voices both gave her courage and submerged any untoward emittances. Erté thought it best not to attend the supper party. The next morning Madame Walska telephoned to inquire after his absence. He explained cautiously, referring with regret to the audience's reaction. 'Oh,' she exclaimed, 'You mean it wasn't a success.'

The most important product of Ganna Walska's ambitions was the collection of Erté's costume designs which lined the walls of her apartment on the Rue de Lubeck when she later directed the Théâtre de Champs Elysées. Eventually she retired to California and presented the drawings and original costumes, made by Redfern, to the Los Angeles County Museum of Art.

In the 'twenties Erté also produced costumes for three famous prima-donnas—Maria Kouznetsov (fig. 164), one of his St Petersburg favourites, the Spanish soprano Lucrezia Bori (fig. 165), who wore his dresses at the Metropolitan Opera, New York, and the beautiful American singer Mary Garden (fig. 157). Many years later he was to design costumes for Vittoria de los Angeles.

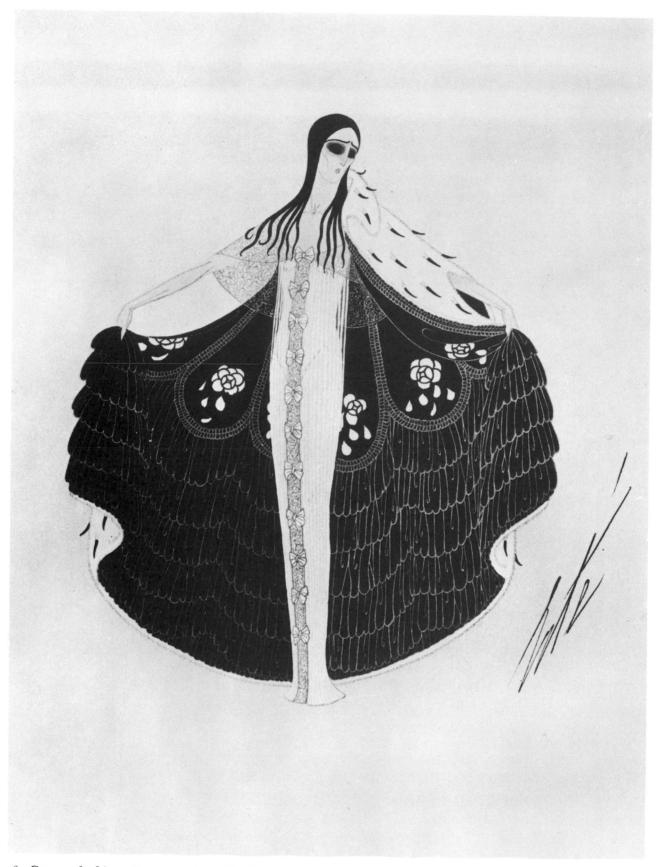

164 Costume for Maria Kouznetsov in *La Traviata*, 1923

In 1921–22 he created costumes for another childhood idol, Pavlova (figs. 167, 168). One of his greatest regrets is that when the opportunity came to work for Diaghilev other commitments interfered. It appears that the décor and costumes for *The Sleeping Beauty* had been left in London after the *Ballets Russes* season of 1921. For various reasons Diaghilev was forced to sell them, although he was contracted to produce the ballet in Paris. It was arranged for him to meet Erté in Monte Carlo, through a mutual friend Princess Tenichof, famous for her centre of modern folkloric art in St Petersburg (see bibliography). Erté made some costume drawings (figs. 170, 171) but eventually had to withdraw because of pressure from *Harper's Bazar* and the theatre. (As a compromise Diaghilev arranged for the last act to be danced in Paris, with the additions of the Russian and Chinese dances from *Casse Noisette*, under the title of *Le Mariage d'Aurore*. He used scenery and costumes from *Le Pavillon d'Armide*, with some new designs by Gontcharova.)

It would require a separate study to discuss Erté's career as an operatic designer over a period of thirty-five years.* He has worked principally in Paris—for the Opéra and the Opéra-Comique, as well as on a series of operettas for Opéra-Bouffe. Abroad he has collaborated with the Riga Opera, San Carlo in Naples, Rouen Opera, the Opéra de Monte Carlo and the Colon Theatre in Buenos Aires. Special mention should be made of his designs for the centenary performance of *Don Pasquale* at the Palais de Chaillot in 1945, and the 1951 production of *La Traviata* at the Paris Opéra to mark the fiftieth anniversary of the death of Verdi. In 1947 he was commissioned for the first performance of Francis Poulenc's setting of Apollinaire's *Les Mamelles de Tirésias* at the Opéra-Comique. In an interview with the French magazine *Opéra* (28 May 1947) the composer explained: 'I asked Erté—the magician of the Bal Tabarin—to design the costumes and décor because for him 1912 is not a reconstruction but a souvenir, since at that time he was in Paris working as a dress designer. Erté has surpassed my expectations and has given a nobility of style to an epoch normally regarded with sarcasm by the younger generation.' (Fig. 122.)

Erté's greatest opera success was probably his last production, *Castor et Pollux* at the Roman theatre, Lyons, in the 1961 Festival (fig. 169). This, as do most operas, still demands the kind of historical fantasy and splendour no longer demanded by the popular musical stage. The skill with which Erté adapted his style to new requirements can be judged by the press reception. 'All is enchantment . . . the richness of the décor, the costumes of the *grand siècle* are extremely luxurious'; thus wrote a Lyons newspaper. 'If there is to be a first compliment,' decided *Paris Soir*, 'it must be to the designer Erté.' *La Croix* agreed: 'If the evening has left us with an unforgettable souvenir the merit is entirely due to Erté the great artist who has realized a veritable fairyland of colour and line in his costumes of an astonishing richness and variety.'

---

* Interested readers will find the artist's interview with the present author in the London magazine *Opera*, September 1967.

165 Costume for Lucrezia Bori in the opera *Pelléas et Mélisande*, 1927

166 Decor for *Don Pasquale*, 1934

167 Gavotte costume for Pavlova, c. 1921

168 Autumn costume for Pavlova, c. 1921

169 Costume for Jupiter in the opera *Castor et Pollux*, 1961

170 & 171 Costumes for Prince Charming and The Lilac Fairy, c. 1921

Ballet, in a sense, was a less revolutionary step in his career since his work for revue was always related to mime, dance and movement. As mentioned earlier, in St Petersburg he had created imaginary ballets. But, apart from the costumes he made for Pavlova and the tentative designs for Diaghilev in the 'twenties, it was much later that he worked on complete ballets. The most important are *La Mère L'Oie*, to the music of Ravel, for the Opéra-Comique and *Self Portrait* for Colonel de Basil's company, both in 1948, and a work commissioned in 1949 by the Marquis de Cuevas, *The Enchanted Mill*. In 1960 he designed a group of ballet films made by Louis Cuny with the dancer Attilio Labis.

His work in opera and ballet alone would have made a full career for many designers. The latest productions, notably *Castor et Pollux* show him in complete command of all the qualities which enabled him to achieve distinction in most other theatrical forms.

In recent years he has also displayed a somewhat unexpected curiosity over new artistic techniques, mastering them with all his usual skill. In the early 'sixties he began to make sculptures called *formes picturales* (fig. 113) out of sheet-metal, decorated with oil pigments. They were first shown at Galerie Ror Volmar, Paris in 1964.

The exhibitions of his designs which took place in Paris, Milan, New York and London in 1966 and 1967 were quite unexpected by the artist. 'It has been like a dream,' he said recently, 'I never imagined that so many people would again be interested in my drawings.' Since then there have been a series of new exhibitions in the United States and Canada, in France, Italy and Germany. He has been commissioned by fashion magazines and theatrical producers for new designs; Alan Aldridge requested a drawing for his book *The Beatles Illustrated* and when Anthony Blond decided to publish Lytton Strachey's mildly risqué tale *Ermyntrude and Esmeralda* he turned to Erté as the ideal illustrator (fig. 175). A remarkable development for a man in his late eighties, perhaps in response to a new public, has been his first albums of lithographs on such typical themes as Numbers, Jewels and Seasons (figs. 172, 173).

In the final stage of preparing this book, Erté was preoccupied with costumes for Zizi Jeanmairc in Roland Petit's recreation of the spectacular French revue at the Casino de Paris. Alongside the couturier Yves Saint Laurent, who is young enough to be his grandson, and such famous *avant-garde* artists as Vasarely, César and Soto, Erté impassively reinterpreted two of his classic motifs—Furs and Diamonds (figs. 174, 177). The show opened in January 1970, in the artist's seventy-eight year, the same month as he was honoured by the French Government by being appointed a Chevalier du Mérite, Artistique et Culturel.

172 'Autumn', 1970

174 Diamond set, 1970

173 'Amethyst', 1969

175 Illustration for *Ermyntrude and Esmeralda,* 1969

176 *Hearts,* design for a lithograph, 1970

177 Costume design for the *Roland Petit Revue*, 1970

NOTES ON ILLUSTRATIONS

Except where stated, Erté's works are either in his own possession or in that of his agent, Grosvenor Gallery, London. The artist retains the copyright over the reproduction of his work.
The medium for the drawings is pen and ink; for the more elaborate theatrical designs, gouache and metallic paint.
All measurements are in inches.

1 The Tirtoff family on holiday in 1905 at Pavlovsk near St Petersburg. Romain, aged thirteen years, stands beside his mother. His father, in naval uniform, is between his sister Nathalia and Madame Tirtoff.

2 Romain de Tirtoff, aged seven years, at the 1900 Paris Exhibition.

3 Graduation photograph taken at Kronstadt in 1911.

4 Design for an imaginary ballet, c. 1911. 12¾ × 9.
The imagery relates to the work of Gustav Moreau and Aubrey Beardsley, whose work the nineteen-year-old artist had seen in Russia. The artist is already using gouache with gold and silver metallic paint, which have remained his principal media.

5 Design for an imaginary ballet, c. 1911. 9¾ × 12½.
Prototype of the artist's oriental fantasies. The grotesque and erotic elements became more restrained when he later designed for the French theatre.

6 Pencil sketches done in St Petersburg after Paul Poiret's visit to the city, c. 1911.
Note the feathered head-dresses, the tubular line and the harem trousers introduced by the couturier, for whom Erté was later to work in Paris.

7 Page from *Harper's Bazar*, January 1915, showing Poiret dress designs, actually drawn by Erté.
Collection Mrs John Whibley, London.

8, 9 These drawings provide a rare opportunity to examine the development of Erté's style. The first design for an evening coat done at Poiret's in 1913 reflects the couturier's luxurious style. The second drawing is the same design redrawn for reproduction in *Harper's Bazar c*. 1915.

10 Oriental costume for Mata Hari in *Le Minaret*, Théâtre de la Renaissance, February 1913. 12¼ × 9¼.

11 La Muse Cubiste for the revue *Plus Ça Change*, 1914. 12½ × 9½.

12 Costume design for *Le Tango*, 1913, reproduced from *La Revue Française, Politique et Littéraire*.

13 Illustration for *Le Ruban* reproduced from *Gazette du Bon Ton*, May 1913.
Probably the first appearance of Erté's signature in a French publication.

14 The second cover for *Harper's Bazar*, November 1915.

15 Page from *Harper's Bazar*, January 1916.

16 *Oiseau du Nord*, 1916. 9¼ × 6¼.
A design for an American fashion house or for *Harper's Bazar*.

17 *Le Silencieux, c.* 1916.
Private collection.
Violet velvet evening coat trimmed with black fur and gold embroidery.

18 *J'en ai Rêvé, c.* 1916. 9 × 6.
Private collection.
White velvet coat over black skirt, with silver decoration and white fur collar.

19, 20 Dress and coat designs for Mrs William Randolph Hearst, 1921. Each 11½ × 10.
Collection Martin Battersby, Brighton, England.
In the *Daily Eagle*, New York, February 1925,

Erté is quoted: 'For Mrs William Randolph Hearst I planned a gown in silver cloth—blueish silver, greenish silver, mauve-silver. With it she wears a coat of silver with stripeings of grey fur.'

21 'Erté writes his own biography.'
Page from *Harper's Bazar*, March 1919.

22 Muff, $4\frac{1}{2} \times 2\frac{3}{4}$.
Harper's Bazar, October 1922: 'Made of otter. Held in the middle by a piece of ermine that forms a bag closed by rings of otter.'

23, 24 Two bathing costumes for *Woman's Home Journal*, 1922. Each $8 \times 5\frac{1}{2}$.

25 *Chapeau Eventail*, $3\frac{1}{2} \times 2\frac{3}{4}$.
Private collection.
Harper's Bazar, July 1921: 'How delightfully convenient on a torrid afternoon to be able to lift one's hat from its foundation and to use it as a fan.'

26 Two masks for *Harper's Bazar*, 1921.
Private collection.

27 Three designs for arm jewelry for *Harper's Bazar*
April 1922: 'A series of onyx bracelets and a long silk tassel to match one's gown.'
'Black and white jade bracelets are linked with black and white jade beads. The earrings and necklace are one.'

28 Head-dress, *Harper's Bazar*, 1921.

29 Hatpin designs for *Harper's Bazar*.

30 *Chapeau pour le soleil*, *Harper's Bazar* 1922: 'Long curling flues (sic) of white ostrich flecked with green jade and attached to a bandeau of jade green beads.'

31 *L'Eventail—Face à Main d'Erté*, 1922. $8\frac{1}{2} \times 7\frac{3}{4}$.
Illustration for *Harper's Bazar*.

32 Comb, $3\frac{1}{2} \times 1\frac{1}{2}$
Harper's Bazar, September 1922: 'An enormous tortoiseshell comb is thrust into the back of a tightly wound gold cloth turban.'

33 Comb, $3 \times 1\frac{1}{2}$.
Harper's Bazar, January 1924: 'The tassel held in the beaks of the two ivory birds that form this comb may be changed to match one's gown.'

34 Frontispiece, *Harper's Bazar*, July 1922.

35 Photograph of Lilian Fisher, who became the Paris Editor of *Harper's Bazar*, wearing a costume in the Greenwich Village Follies of 1922, based on the above.

36 *The Unfeeling Heart*.
Harper's Bazar cover, April 1918: 'The En-chantress in the white tent, draped in her magenta scarf, rapidly appraises her coiffure in the mirror of her little powder box. A puff in her hand, with cold unconcern she makes ready to powder her face—while to the death struggle taking place behind the tent she is calmly indifferent.'

37 *Love's Captive*, $14\frac{1}{2} \times 10\frac{3}{4}$.
Original design for the *Harper's Bazar* cover December 1921.

38 *Harper's Bazar* cover, 1924.
This marks the change from allegorical designs.

39 *Harper's Bazaar* cover, April 1930.
The influence of Cubism and jazz.

40 *Harper's Bazaar* cover, October 1933.
Simplified geometrical patterns and the return to a longer, more feminine, line.

41 *Harper's Bazaar* cover, May 1935.
A modernistic design in complete contrast to the early oriental and anecdotal styles.

42, 43 Double page from *Harper's Bazar*, September 1920, including Erté's letter from Monte Carlo.

44 Evening gown, $9\frac{1}{2} \times 6$.
Harper's Bazar, July 1917: 'Coral beads form embroidered motifs on an artistic evening gown of heavy white satin. The ends of smoke-grey chiffon are caught to the coral strands that hold the bodice in place and form a butterfly bow.'

45 *Pour le Promenade*, $11 \times 6\frac{1}{2}$
Harper's Bazar, April 1918: 'The mode suggests that the hat and girdle match and Erté expands the idea and adds gauntlets and parasol cover. His selection of chamois cloth is practical.'

46 Fringed and beaded evening coat, 10×7.
Private collection.
Appeared in *Harper's Bazar*, March 1921.

47 Designs for mink capes, 1921.
Each $13\frac{1}{4} \times 9\frac{1}{4}$.
Privately commissioned.

48 Erté at the Bal du Grand Prix, Paris Opéra, 1926.
For this ball he also designed a Velasquez costume for the Infante Don Luis of Spain. They were both attendants to the Marchesa Casati who appeared as la Castiglione.

49 Erté in a costume worn at the Monte Carlo Sporting Club.
Described in *Harper's Bazar*, May 1923: 'I was dressed as a Momie, covered by a black and red envelope with openings for eye and mouth. I was led through the room by an Egyptian slave. The wrappings were then taken off by the slave and, freed from the golden cape wrapped round my body, I appeared in the costume of an Egyptian Pharaoh. Among the

demons and pyjamas my costume was much appreciated.'

50 Erté at a fancy-dress ball at the Monte Carlo Sporting Club.
Described in *Harper's Bazar*, June 1922: 'At the Ball only white silk or white velvet costumes were allowed. Mine was entirely made of *lamé d'argent*, ornamented with a multitude of pearls. I christened it "Clair de Lune" as in this costume there is nothing oriental but my own imagination. The first prize was awarded to "Clair de Lune" which was noticeable, even in the blaze of the electric light, among the other original costumes.'

51 Drawing reproduced in *Costume Design and Illustration*, New York 1918.
The original illustration appeared in *Harper's Bazar*, December 1916: with the following caption: 'Striking indeed on the bridle path will be "l'Amazone du Demain" in a suit of grey chamois with a cardigan of blue silk. The gaiters which are one with the breeches fasten with conspicuous blue buttons. Erté's "Promenade Matinale" is a striking habit of beige cloth with breeches cut in one with the skirt of the coat. The black silk stock wraps about the neck and is knotted in the front.'

52 Evening dress, $11\frac{3}{4} \times 8\frac{1}{4}$.
Harper's Bazar, October 1924: 'This evening robe is shaded from a vivid green skirt to a white bodice.'

53 Drawing, $2\frac{1}{2} \times 5\frac{1}{2}$.
Frontispiece for *Harper's Bazar*, August 1923: 'One of the symbols of life is reflected in her eyes; she sees it but is not frightened for it is only a butterfly suggesting in its flight the constant movement of life.'

54 Dress designs for *Woman's Home Journal*, 1924. Each 11×9.

55 Pyjama suit, 1922. 9×5.
Private collection.
Pale mauve pyjamas trimmed in green. Note the RT at neckline. The pocket repeats the tassel motif at the belt.

56 'Silhouettes 1925–8'. Gouache. $11 \times 7\frac{3}{4}$.
One of the illustrations for Erté's article on *Modern Dress* in The Encyclopaedia Brittanica, 1929.

57 'Modern sports dress for men and women', $11 \times 7\frac{1}{2}$.
Illustration for *Encyclopaedia Britannica*, 1929.

58 Two costumes for *La Fête de St Cyr*, 1915. Each $9\frac{1}{4} \times 6$.

59 Costume for *Les Amazones*, Ba-ta-Clan Theatre, Paris 1916. $10 \times 6\frac{3}{4}$.
Collection W.T.Jarosz, London.

60 The Caliph's Favourite in 'The Thousand and Second Night at Baghdad', for *L'Orient Merveilleux*, Fémina Theatre, Paris 1917. $10\frac{1}{4} \times 7\frac{1}{2}$.
Collection M.Moross, South Africa.

61 Costume for Mistinguett in the revue *L'Orient Merveilleux*, Fémina Theatre, Paris 1917. 15×10.
Collection Mrs S.M.Drage, London.
The cloak is in midnight blue with green and gold appliqué and gold and silver tassels. The pearl helmet bears rays of blue and green aigrettes.

62 Diamond Statue in 'The Thousand and Second Night at Baghdad', for *L'Orient Merveilleux*, Fémina Theatre, Paris 1917. 10×7.
Private collection.
The whole costume is made of strung beads in a series of spiders' webs with scroll designs.

63 The Genie of the Lamp in 'The Thousand and Second Night at Baghdad', for *L'Orient Merveilleux*, Fémina Theatre, Paris 1917. 10×7.
Private collection.
The gold lamé trousers cover the feet, and the pearl waist fringe extends to anklets. The gold filigree stomacher and bodice are joined to a head-dress of silver and pearl rays.

64 Cactus costume for 'Fleur du Mal', in the revue *Gobette de Paris*, Ba-ta-Clan theatre, Paris 1917. $9\frac{1}{4} \times 5\frac{3}{4}$.
See-through costume and boots in silver mesh, decorated with ruby fringes.

65 Venetian costume, Folies-Bergère, 1919.
Present ownership unknown.
One of the first costumes which Erté designed for the Folies-Bergère.

66 Starfish in *Fonds de la Mer*, Folies-Bergère, 1919. 15×11.
Private collection.

67 Messalina, Apollo Theatre, Paris, 1923. 15×11.
A splendid statuesque figure reminiscent of the *Bal des Arts* designs of 1919. The gown is a sequence of pink, orange and red, ending in black and gold. Silver and blue beads on the arms, looped to the ears. The golden Roman coiffure has a silver and blue cap.

68 Curtain design for *Conte Hindou*, Folies-Bergère, 1922. $10 \times 13\frac{3}{4}$.
Two curtains, each with five Negroes; an early example of Erté's 'living curtains'.

69 Costume, *Conte Hindou*, Folies-Bergère, 1922. $12\frac{1}{2} \times 9\frac{1}{2}$.
Collection Chiu, London.

70 Costume, *Conte Hindou*, Folies-Bergère, 1922.
Present ownership unknown.

71 Evening coat for Bendels, New York, *c.* 1916. 9¼ × 6¼.

72 *Splendeur*, evening gown for Bendels, New York, *c.* 1916. 9½ × 6.
The artist regards this as his favourite fashion design.

73 Erté's first cover for *Harper's Bazar*, January 1915.

74 *La Toilette de la Nature*, 16 × 11.
Galleria Milano, Milan, Italy.
Original design for the *Harper's Bazar* cover, October 1920: 'Nature changes her costume each season, but quite without cost, whereas with the fair sex. . . .'

75 One of the Three Wise Kings for 'Les Rois des Légendes', in *La Marche à l'Etoile*, Fémina Theatre, Paris 1919. 13½ × 9½.
Collection Mrs S.M.Drage, London.

76 One of the Negro figures in the *Conte Hindou* curtain, Folies Bergère, 1922. 13¾ × 10¼

77 Plume, costume for Max Weldy, 1920, 12 × 9½.
Private collection.

78 *The Treasures of Indo-China*, L'Alcazar de Marseilles, 1922. 21½ × 29½.

79 Venetian Courtesan, Folies-Bergère, 1923. 15¾ × 11¼.

80 Schéhérazade décor for *Aladin*, Folies-Bergère, 1929. 14½ × 18½.

81 Wedding costume, *Aladin*, Folies-Bergère, 1929. 14½ × 10¾.

82 Melisande's attendant, *La Princesse Lointaine* by Edmond Rostand, Sarah Bernhardt Theatre, Paris, 1929. 15¼ × 11.

83 The Golden Calf in *Les Idoles*, Folies-Bergère, 1924.
Present ownership unknown.

84 Vestale, *Les Idoles*, Folies-Bergère, 1924. 10 × 6.
Private collection

85 Aphrodite, *Les Idoles*, Folies-Bergère, 1924.
Present ownership unknown.
Reproduced with Erté's essay on costume design in the *Encyclopaedia Brittanica*, 1929.

86 *Les Bijoux de Perles*, Folies-Bergère, 1924.
Present ownership unknown.
Metro Goldwyn-Mayer bought copies of the costumes for this ballet for the film *Paris* (see fig. 136).

87 Lotus, *The Treasures of Indo-China*, L'Alcazar de Marseilles, 1922. 15½ × 11.

Green and silver skirt with a gold and pearl bodice. Head-dress and jewels in gold.

88 Mother of Pearl Ballet, *The Treasures of Indo-China*, L'Alcazar de Marseilles, 1922. 24 × 14.
The dancer sits in an oyster shell borne by two attendants in costumes of blue, green, orange, mauve and gold. The dancer wears a pale green skirt decorated by pearls, and a gold pagoda head-dress.

89 The Kiss of the Courtesan, *Les Baisers*, Fémina Theatre, Paris 1921.
Present ownership unknown.
The man's Russian costume and the similarity between the woman's exotic costume and Erté's youthful designs in 1911, refer back to his early years in St Petersburg.

90 The Maternal Kiss, *Les Baisers*, Fémina Theatre, Paris 1921. 11 × 15.
Erté seems to have been fascinated by the possibilities of the crinoline skirt. A notable example is the cover for *Harper's Bazar* for February 1918 where a lover hides in the skirt.

91 Costume for *Le Sphinx* by Maurice Rostand, Sarah Bernhardt Theatre, 1924. 15¼ × 11¼.
The head-dress is in gold and green, the cloak blue and green and the gown gold with mauve decorations. 'Gilda Darthy asked me to design the costume of the Sphinx and also the dresses. It gave me the greatest pleasure to be permitted to design the costume of the Sphinx, explaining all the mystery of that fabulous monster. This costume was altogether the antithesis of the music-hall *vedette* costume of Madame (Ida) Rubinstein.' Erté, in *Harper's Bazar*, May 1924.

92 The Sultan, *Aladin*, Folies-Bergère, 1929. 10¾ × 9½.
Present ownership unknown.

93 The Devil, *La Femme et le Diable*, originally for the Apollo Theatre, Paris 1923 and later at the Winter Garden, New York. 12 × 9½.
Black and white costume with a silver snake-belt at the waist with a red tassel as its tongue. Note repetition on the turban.

94, 95 La Bergère de France and her Page, *La Femme et le Diable*, originally for the Apollo Theatre, Paris 1923 and later at the Winter Garden, New York. 14 × 9½ and 12¼ × 9¼.
Each lady was accompanied by two pages; an early version of collective costumes.

96 The Arctic Sea, *George White's Scandals*, New York 1925. 15 × 11.
Collection, Charles Spencer, London.
From the stalactite head-dress rows of pearls descend together with silver drapes to simulate a torrent of icy water.

97 Spirals costume, *George White's Scandals*, New York 1925. 11 × 15.
The tunic in gold and purple; extended green

and gold sleeve with spiral motif, repeated on arm and leg.

98 Charleston, *George White's Scandals*, New York 1925. 14½ × 11.
The Metropolitan Museum of Art, New York
This costume introduced the dance to the American stage. Note the typically witty use of the triple image—the shadow presumably painted on the curtain and the costume repeating the outline of the figure.

99 Black Bottom, *George White's Scandals*, New York 1925. 15 × 11.
Collection Cecil Beaton, London.
This dance was said to have been invented by George White and created by Ann Pennington.

100 The Handbag, *George White's Scandals*, New York 1926.
Collection Gunter Sachs, Paris.
Maurice Feuillet wrote: 'Can one imagine anything more exquisite than this handbag of diamonds suspended by strings of pearls? The clasp consists of two women nonchalantly reclining their ivory bodies adorned with tunics of flexible links entwined with pearls.' *Le Gaulois Artistique*, nos 33–34, 1929.

101 Curtain for 'The Golden Fables', *George White's Scandals*, New York, 1926.
Collection Tessa Kennedy, London.

102 Costume, 'The Golden Fables', *George White's Scandals*, 1926.
Present ownership unknown.
A typical example of Erté's humour. The image was used again in a lithograph (fig. 181) and in the Diamond scene for the Casino de Paris 1970 (fig. 179).

103 Slave costume, Apollo Theatre, Paris, 1921. 13 × 9¼.
The stiffened transparent skirt is decorated in gold with an orange tassel from the silver belt. Another orange tassel descends from the elaborate turban.

104 Moods, *George White's Scandals*, 1926.
Present ownership unknown.
Figures designed to appear in the eyes of the mask represented Love, Jealousy, Sadness and Indifference.

105 The Guadalquivir, *The Rivers*, Folies-Bergère, 1923. 14 × 20.
Victoria and Albert Museum, London.
This series of designs together with those for 'The Seas' (*George White's Scandals*), now in the Metropolitan Museum, New York, represent the final elaboration of the collective costume.

106 The Nile, *George White's Scandals*, New York 1925. 10½ × 14½.
This design was for a second series of rivers done for Broadway.

107 Silk, Folies-Bergère, 1927. 15½ × 25.
Victoria and Albert Museum, London.
Exhibited in the Exhibition *Les Années 25*, Musée des Arts Décoratifs, Paris 1966.

108 Perfumes, Folies-Bergère, 1927. 22¼ × 16.
A suspended girl as the living part of an architectural structure.

109 Setting for a Fancy Dress Ball, 1919. 16 × 16.
Collection Susannah York, London.
This setting and a series of fancy-dress costumes were commissioned by William Randolph Hearst for the film *Restless Sex*, starring Marion Davies and directed by Robert Z.Leonard, released in December 1920.

110 Zeus, for the film *Restless Sex*, 1919. 14½ × 13.
Collection Susannah York, London.

111 Costume for Ganna Walska for the opera *Zaza*, 1920. 12½ × 11.

112 Décor, *Les Mamelles de Tirésias*, Opéra-Comique. Paris 1947. 14¾ × 10¾.

113 Perpetuum Mobile, 1961. Aluminium and oil paint 11½ h × 14½ × 20.

114 Poster for Theodore Kosloff's Ballet School in Hollywood. 15½ × 12.
Collection Susannah York, London.
The poster was designed in Monte Carlo at the request of Theodore Kosloff's wife before Erté went to Hollywood in 1925. Stylized lettering in the form of human bodies was later used for an alphabet designed in 1932 and in some of the lithographs of 1969–70.

115 Diamonds and Attendants for 'The Treasures', *George White's Scandals*, New York, 1926. 15 × 11.
Collection Charles Spencer, London.
The eclectic mixture of Russian Orthodox motifs, the almost Minoan costumes of the attendants, plus the *Art Deco* decorations on their legs, is typical of Erté's work of this period.

116 The Kiss of Fire, *Les Baisers*, Fémina Theatre, Paris 1921.
Present ownership unknown.
A simple example of a collective costume for two figures—also an early version of Unisex clothes.

117 Curtain for an African Ballet, *George White's Scandals*, New York, 1924. 26 × 36.
The Museum of Modern Art, New York.
Reproduced with Erté's article on Costume Design in the *Encyclopaedia Britannica*, 1929. The end papers of this book are taken from this curtain design.

118 Diamond Curtain for 'The Treasures', *George White's Scandals*, New York, 1925. 16 × 10.
Collection Lex Aitken, London.
An elaborate variation of a design using suspended girls.

119 One of the figures in the African Ballet Curtain (fig. 117)
Present ownership unknown.

120 Indian Dagger Dance Curtain, *George White's Scandals*, New York, 1928. 11 × 15.
Two costume designs are in the Metropolitan Museum, New York.

121 Opening Curtain, *Manhattan Mary*, Majestic Theatre, New York, 1927. 11 × 16.
A number of other designs for this musical comedy are in the Metropolitan Museum, New York.

122 Snakeskin Curtain, *Manhattan Mary*, Majestic Theatre, New York. 15½ × 11.

123 Onion costume, Vegetable Ballet, *George White's Scandals*, New York 1926. 15¼ × 11.

124 Potato costume, Vegetable Ballet, *George White's Scandals*, New York 1926. 15¼ × 11.

125 The Sultan, for the film *Restless Sex*, 1919. 10¾ × 9½.
The black and silver patterned coat has a reverse design in emerald green and gold seen on the sleeves.

126 Yacodhara, for the film *Restless Sex*, 1919. 14 × 11.
Collection Susannah York, London.

127 Erté in his studio at Sèvres, 1924.
This room was reproduced by MGM for Erté's use at Culver City in 1925.

128, 129 Costume for Carmel Myers in the film *Ben Hur* (present ownership unknown) and a photograph of Erté with the actress in 1925.

130 Costume for Aileen Pringle in the film *The Mystic*, 1925.
Present ownership unknown.

131, 132 Costume for Aileen Pringle in the film *The Mystic* (present ownership unknown) and a photograph of the actress.

133 Gypsy costume for Aileen Pringle in the film *The Mystic*, 1925. 14½ × 10½
Collection Susannah York, London.

134-135 Costume for Norma Shearer in the fashion revue 'Her Day' staged in Los Angeles 20 April 1925 (present ownership unknown), and a photograph of the actress.

136 Evening coat for Aileen Pringle in the film *Dance Madness*, 1925. 15 × 11¼.
Collection Susannah York, London.
The coat is trimmed with white and black fox furs and gold embroidery. Note the adder's head motif at the end of the sleeves and on the helmet.

137 Costume for the film *Dance Madness*, directed by Robert Z. Leonard, 1925. 15 × 11.
Collection Susannah York, London.
Compare with early beaded costume fig. 62, and fig. 118 for *George White's Scandals*.

138 Dressing-room for the film *A Little Bit of Broadway*, 1925. 10 × 11¼.
Collection Susannah York, London.
The furniture and doors are lavender, the walls grey, the dados and carpet black, the bowl of flowers brilliant vermilion.

139 Costume for the film *Time The Comedian*, 1925. 15¼ × 11¼.
Formerly in the collection of Susannah York, present ownership unknown.
The repetition of motifs is a popular device of the artist. He used this idea for a cover for *Harper's Bazar*, June 1927.

140 Ballet costume for the film *Time The Comedian*, directed by Robert Z. Leonard, 1925. 15¼ × 11¼.
Collection Susannah York, London.
The theme of the film is indicated by one hand in the form of a clock and the other as Father Time.

141-2 Costumes for Mimi (Lillian Gish) and Musette (Renée Adorée) in the film *La Bohème*, directed by King Vidor, 1925. Each 15¼ × 11¼.
Formerly in the collection of Susannah York.

143 Boudoir for the film *Paris*, 1925. 13¾ × 21½.
Collection Susannah York, London.

144 Night-club for the film *Paris*, 1925. 13 × 21½.
Collection Susannah York, London.
The walls and floor are red, the dado red and gold and the furniture black and gold.

145 Costume for Belgium in the Prologue at the première of *The Big Parade*, Grauman's Egyptian Theatre, 1925. 15¼ × 11¼.
Collection Susannah York, London.
'The prologue included a stage review of the greater allied nations and America . . . designed by Monsieur Romain de Tirtoff Erté. . . . Belgium with an enormous silver sword piercing her head from the top and issuing from the body at the waist from which a blood red color flowed. . . .', *State Journal*, Columbus, Ohio, 15 November 1925.

146 Costume for the Bal Tabarin, Paris, *c.* 1936. 14½ × 10½.
Typical of the costumes designed for this revue between 1933 and 1952, and the return to a long, flowing feminine line.

177

147 Costume for Cecile Sorel, ABC Theatre, *Paris*, 1935. 14½ × 10½.
The famous actress appeared in a sketch as Madame du Barry.

148 Aztec Ballet costume, *It's in the Bag*, Saville Theatre, London 1937. 14½ × 10¾.
Collection Michael Patmore, Lewes, England.

149 Set for *It's in the Bag*, Saville Theatre, London 1937. 10½ × 14½.

150 Samson and Delilah in 'Famous Heroines', *George White's Scandals*, New York 1926. Later presented as *Les Princesses de la Légende* at the Folies-Bergère.
Present ownership unknown.
This is probably the finest of Erté's designs in which he uses huge sculptural figures.

151 The Golden Calf for 'The Golden Fables', *George White's Scandals*, New York, 1926. 15½ × 17½.
Galleria Milano, Milan, Italy.
This magnificent design forms the centrepiece of the elaborate curtain in fig. 101.

152 Sisters Curtain, *George White's Scandals*, New York, 1926. Later used by the Dolly Sisters at the Casino de Paris. 10¼ × 15½.
Galleria Milano, Milan, Italy.
Another example of Erté's witty repetition of design elements.

153 Costume, *Manhattan Mary*, Majestic Theatre, New York, 1927. 11 × 10¼.
Private collection.
This design originally appeared as a black and white fashion illustration in *Harper's Bazar*, March 1921.

154 Hera, for the film *Restless Sex*, 1919. 14½ × 13.
Collection Susannah York, London.

155 Setting for an oriental ballet in the film *Paris*, 1925. 12 × 16.
Collection Susannah York, London.

156 Dining-room for the film *Paris*, 1925. 15 × 21½.
Collection Susannah York, London.

157 Costume for Mary Garden in *L'Amore dei Tre Re*, 1926. 19 × 12.
Galleria Milano, Milan, Italy.

158 Directoire costume, *Au Temps des Merveilleuses*, Théâtre du Chatelet, Paris, 1934. 14½ × 10½.
Transparent black dress over yellow tights, with black and silver train. Stole, cap and feathers in orange and yellow.

159 Symphony in Black, *London Symphony*, London Palladium 1938. 14½ × 10½.
Collection Mrs R.W.Beck, New York.

160 Symphony in Grey, *London Symphony*, London Palladium 1938. 14½ × 10½.

161 The Symphony, Bal Tabarin, Paris 1945. 12½ × 9½.
One of a series of costumes representing musical terms.

162 Amazon, *Casanova*, Teatro Calderón, Barcelona, 1945. 14½ × 10½.

163 Costume for Ganna Walska as Gilda in *Rigoletto*, 1920. 14 × 10¾.
Metropolitan Museum, New York.

164 Costume for Maria Kouznetsov as Violetta in *La Traviata*, 1923. 14¼ × 10½.

165 Costume for Lucrezia Bori in *Pelléas et Mélisande*, 1927. 15¾ × 12.
Metropolitan Museum, New York.

166 Décor for *Don Pasquale*, Riga Opera, 1934. 11½ × 19¾.
Erté's first designs for a full-length opera, commissioned by the newly built opera house at Riga and produced in 1935. In 1936 he also designed *Faust* for this company.

167 Gavotte, costume for Pavlova, c. 1921. 14¾ × 10¾.
Collection Mrs A.Norman, London.

168 Autumn, costume for Pavlova, c. 1921. 14¾ × 10¾.
Collection Mrs J.Bennett, London.

169 Costume for Jupiter, *Castor et Pollux*, Festival de Lyon, 1961. 19 × 14¼.

170-1 Costumes for Prince Charming and the Lilac Fairy for the ballet *The Sleeping Beauty*, c. 1921. 14¾ × 10¾.
These designs were made for Diaghilev.

172 Autumn, from a set of four lithographs *The Four Seasons*. 25¼ × 19½.
Published by the Grosvenor Gallery, London 1970.

173 Amethyst, from a set of six lithographs of *Precious Stones*. 25¼ × 19½.
Published by the Grosvenor Gallery, London 1969.

174 Diamond set for the *Roland Petit Revue*, Casino de Paris, 1970. 11¾ × 7.

175 Illustration for *Ermyntrude and Esmeralda* by Lytton Strachey, published by Anthony Blond, London 1969.

176 Hearts, a design for a set of lithographs based on playing cards. 1970. 25¼ × 19½.

177 Costume design for the *Roland Petit Revue*, Casino de Paris, 1970. 14½ × 11.

SELECTED BIBLIOGRAPHY

CHAPTER 2

Fen, Elisaveta *A Russian Childhood*. Methuen, London 1961

Fr-Chirovsky, Nicholas L. *An Introduction to Russian History*. Philosophical Library, New York 1967

Gosling, Nigel *Leningrad*. Studio Vista, London 1965

Gray, Camilla *The Great Experiment: Russian Art 1863–1922*. Thames and Hudson, London 1962

Haskell, Arnold *Diaghilev*. Gollancz, London 1955

Lieven, Prince Peter *The Birth of the Ballets Russes*. Allen & Unwin, London 1965

Lifar, Serge *Diaghilev*. Putnam, London 1940

Maugham, W.Somerset *A Writer's Notebook*. Heinemann, London 1949

Rice, Tamara Talbot *Russian Art*. Thames and Hudson, London 1965

Tuluchniko: L'Art Décoratif des Ateliers de la Princesse Tenichof. Introduction by N.Roerich. St Petersburg 1906

CHAPTER 3

Battersby, Martin *The Decorative Twenties*. Studio Vista, London 1969

Broby-Johansen, R. *Body and Clothes*. Faber, London 1968

Comœdia Illustré, Paris. Monthly issues 1912–1925

Crespelle, Jean-Paul *La Folle Epoque: Des Ballets Russes au Surréalisme*. Hachette, Paris 1968

Gazette du Bon Ton, Paris. Monthly issues 1913–23.

Gernsheim, Alison *Fashion and Reality 1870–1917*. Faber, London 1963

Laver, James *A Concise History of Costume*. Thames and Hudson, London 1969

Poiret, Paul *My First Fifty Years*. Gollancz, London 1931

Tolstoy, Mary Koutousou *Charlemagne to Dior: The History of French Fashion*. Slain Publications, 1967

CHAPTER 4

Coblentz, Edmond D. *William Randolph Hearst: A Portrait in his own Words*. Simon and Shuster, New York 1952

Encyclopaedia Britannica, 14th edition, 1929

Fifty Years of Vogue 1916–1966. Issue of October 1966

Harper's Bazar (or *Bazaar*), American edition. Monthly issues from January 1915

Mott, Frank Luther *A History of American Magazines*, Vol. 5, 1905–30. Harvard University Press, 1938

Mott, Frank Luther *American Journalism*. Macmillan, New York 1942

Swanberg, W.A. *Citizen Hearst*. Longmans Green, London 1962

Traphagen, Ethel *Costume Design and Illustrations*. Wiley and Sons, New York and Chapman and Hall, London 1918

Winkler, John K. *William Randolph Hearst: A New Appraisal.* Hastings House, New York 1955

Wood, James Playstead *Magazines in the United States.* Ronald Press, New York 1956

CHAPTER 5

Barrett, Marvin *The Jazz Age.* Putnam, New York 1959

Churchill, Allen *The Great White Way.* Dutton, New York 1962

Damase, Jacques *Les Folies du Music-Hall.* Anthony Blond, London 1962

Derval, Paul *Folies-Bergère.* Les Editions de Paris, 1954

Feschotte, Jacques *Histoire du Music-Hall.* Presses Universitaires de France, Paris 1965

Greer, Howard *Designing Male.* Robert Hale, London 1952

Hughes, Glenn *A History of the American Theatre 1700–1950.* Samuel French 1951

Jacques-Charles *Cent Ans de Music-Hall.* Editions Icheber, Genève-Paris 1956

Laver, James *Costume in the Theatre.* Harrap, London 1964

The Pageant of America: Vol. XIV The American Stage. Yale University Press, 1929

CHAPTER 6

L'Art du Costume dans le Film, *La Revue du Cinéma,* Paris, Autumn 1949

Blum, Daniel *A Pictorial History of the Silent Screen.* Grosset and Dunlop, New York 1953

Brownlow, Kevin *The Parades Gone By.* Secker and Warburg, London 1968

Crowther, Bosley *Hollywood Rajah: The Life and Times of Louis B. Mayer.* Hart Rinehart and Winston, New York 1960

French, Philip *The Movie Moguls.* Weidenfeld and Nicholson, London 1969

Gish, Lilian with Ann Pinchet *The Movies, Mr Griffiths and Me.* W.H.Allen, London 1969

Sarris, Andrew *The American Cine Directors and Directors.* Dutton, New York 1969

CHAPTER 7

Les Années '25 Catalogue of the exhibition held at the Musée des Arts Décoratifs. Paris 1966

Barbier, Georges: Catalogues of Erté's exhibitions at the Charpentier Gallery, Paris, and the William E.Cox Gallery, New York, 1929

Catalogues of Erté exhibitions: Galleria Milano, Milan, Italy 1966; Grosvenor Gallery, London 1967; Sears-Vincent Price Gallery, Chicago 1967-8; Follies and Fashions, Metropolitan Museum of Art, New York 1968

Feuillet, Maurice *Le Peintre-Poète Erté,* Le Gaulois Artistique, no. 33/34, Paris 1929

Davis, Ronald *Opera in Chicago: A Social and Cultural History 1850–1968.* Appleton-Century, New York 1968

Veronesi, Giulia *Stile 1925.* Vallecchi Editore, Firenze 1966; Thames and Hudson, London 1969

INDEX

References to illustration numbers and the corresponding notes on pages 172–78 are in bold type.